A Tale of Two Towns
-
Calleva and Reading

The People of Reading

from the

Earliest Times to 1121

John Mullaney

2020

First published 2020

ISBN 978-0-9935512-7-7

Every attempt has been made to contact any holders of copyright for the illustrations used in this book. If we have made any omissions in acknowledging these we would be grateful if you contact us so that this may be rectified in any future reprint.

Jacket design
JRMullaney FSAI

The colours represent the two towns:
red for Reading and green for Calleva.

The word 'Reading' is possibly associated with someone or
something red or fiery.
Calleva may have meant a place in the woods.
The crest is that of Reading Abbey and the coin shows the
three-split-tailed horse of the Atrebates tribe who occupied
Calleva before the arrival of the Romans.

Published by Scallop Shell Press

29 Derby Road,

Caversham,

Reading.

RG4 5HE

FOREWORD

The closure of Reading Gaol in 2012 coincided with Reading Borough Council's bid for Heritage Lottery Fund money, with a view to conserving the crumbling ruins of Reading's ancient Abbey and bringing the whole Abbey Quarter back into the mainstream of the life of the town. The fact that Henry I had been buried at Reading in 1136 was well known; whether his remains were still there was not so clear. Following the discovery, and re-interment, of the remains of Richard III in Leicester, questions began to be asked about the possibility of finding another English king. That Reading Gaol, made famous by its association with Oscar Wilde, was either built next to, or even above, the site of Henry's grave, attracted the attention of the national media and stimulated local interest.

Using the comprehensive archive of illustrations and photographs in Reading Library, I had just completed several years' research looking at the history of Reading's Abbey Quarter. I was fortunate in being able to draw on the dedicated work of David Cliffe in cataloguing these records. In addition I used a variety of historic maps, photographs and archaeological surveys and was guided by the work of Dr. Cecil Slade, Professor Brian Kemp and that invaluable reference book, *A Biographical Dictionary of Architects at Reading,* by Sidney Gold. Consequently, I was able to present the reader with an illustrated story of how the Abbey Quarter had developed over the years following the dissolution of the Abbey in 1539, and published it as *Reading's Abbey Quarter: An Illustrated History.*

I was approached by Philippa Langley, who had spearheaded the quest for Richard III in Leicester, enquiring about Reading Abbey and the reports that Henry I was buried here. We invited Philippa to a meeting with Canon John O'Shea, Parish Priest at St James' Catholic Church, adjacent to the Abbey ruins and the gaol. My wife, Lindsay, joined the group and we discussed the feasibility of further research. This was the start of what was to become the Hidden Abbey Project, (HAP). There was some initial scepticism from many people, who did not believe that English Heritage, (now Historic England), would allow any work, not even non-invasive geophysics, on this sensitive site. Nevertheless, we invited the regional director of English Heritage to meet our small group. When he visited us he was enthusiastic about the Project.

One problem was that the Project was viewed as a hunt for another English king. Many of us, including myself, were very doubtful about whether Henry's remains were still *in situ*. When it became clear that the Hidden Abbey Project was primarily aimed at discovering the true extent of this ancient Abbey, key figures in Reading Borough Council agreed to, and indeed encouraged, a wider research project than that already underway in connection with the Lottery Fund bid. The Mayor for 2015-2016, Councillor Sarah Hacker, and Councillor Tony Page, Deputy Leader of the Council, were not just enthusiastic supporters, but became the main driving force behind HAP.

The Project's first aim, therefore, was to discover the extent of the Abbey by means of ground penetrating radar. It was hoped that this would not just determine the size of the Abbey but would also reveal more about its nature, without the necessity of invasive archaeology. Historic England supported this aim and even agreed to keyhole trenching, if the results warranted such a move.

Whilst writing and researching *Reading's Abbey Quarter,* I became increasingly fascinated about why Henry had chosen Reading to be the site of his mausoleum, with the intention that it should become, not just his final resting place, but also that of all his heirs. In short, had this happened, Reading would have become one of England's most important towns, if not a major city.

To answer this question, I decided to look back into the town's origins and trace its development up to the founding of the Benedictine monastery in 1121. Strictly speaking, the Abbey was founded in 1123; before this date it was a priory.

This is the story of that journey. I did not know, when I started, whether there would be any clues as to why Henry came to his decision. It is for the reader to interpret the evidence that appears in the following pages. What I offer is a synthesis of many pieces of research from many disciplines. As a syncretic historian, I draw upon the expertise and detailed studies of researchers in many fields, ranging from geology and topography, to archaeology and onomatology, and always with the historian's eye of critical doubt. But most of all I hope to bring together relevant evidence, which both the professional historian, and the interested amateur, may find useful and informative.

A student of history must always expect that more evidence will come to light to confirm, or confound, any current theory. For instance, we believe that we know, to within a few paces, where Henry was buried. Is this really the case?

I hope the reader will enjoy the following look at the town of Reading and the people who have inhabited the area from the earliest times. Although we may never know exactly what was in his mind, I hope these pages will give an insight into why Henry chose Reading, and this part of the town in particular, for his final resting place.

CONTENTS

ACKNOWLEDGEMENTS

I owe a great deal of thanks to the following who advised on their specialisms, making suggestions for improvements to, and correcting, my draft script.

Archaeology - Julia Meen MSc. Oxford Archaeology

Geology - Dr Antoinette Manion, Honorary Fellow of the University of Reading

Medieval French - Dr Philippa Hardman, the University of Reading

Overview - David Cliffe

Petrology - Dr. Kevin Hayward, University of Reading, and Pre-Construct Archaeology Ltd

Proofreading - Lindsay Mullaney MA

Proofreading and the Roman Empire - Hafiz Ladell MA

Saxon Medieval French and Latin Toponomy - Professor Emerita Françoise Le Saux, the University of Reading

LIST OF ABBREVIATED REFERENCES

ASC: *The Anglo-Saxon Chronicle.*

BAJ: *Berkshire Archaeological Journal .*

DBG: Commentarii de Bello Gallico, Julius Caesar, Aulus Hirtius.

ERW: Excavations on Reading Waterfront Sites, 1979 -1988, Hawkes and Fasham, Trust for Wessex Archaeology 1997.

ND: *Notitia Dignitatum.* 5th-6th century document copied in the 15th and 16th century.

RAQ: Reading's Abbey Quarter, John Mullaney, 2014.

UO: *Under the Oracle.* Ford, Poor, Wilkinson, Shaffrey. Oxford Archaeology 2013.

INTRODUCTION

To touch a three-thousand-year-old flint tool, or to hold a hand-written letter from a grandparent, evokes an intimacy with our fellow human beings across time. This is the attraction and power of archaeology. Written history is often at one remove from such intimacy.

In this book, I want the reader to feel a companionship with all those people who have lived in our part of the Thames Valley for over three thousand years.

Who were these people? Like us, they could have stood on the higher land overlooking the Thames and gazed across the great river towards the rolling wooded hills on its northern bank. Or they could have looked down at the swift-flowing waters in flood as they made their way back home to their family, their children, their loved ones.

To help the reader make these connections, I often quote the actual words used by chroniclers, be they in Old English, Latin or Greek, but always with their translation. I ask you to take your time to read these words. It does not matter if you understand each word, or the grammar. Try to let the words get under your skin, to bring you closer to these people, our ancestors.

And they are our ancestors. That is my second aim. I hope to show how we can learn, both from archaeology and from the earliest records in our possession, that this part of the Thames has been home to a continual flow of incomers, many of whom have left their mark: an inheritance which touches on our own lives today.

I will show how even the very name of our town is a conundrum which reflects this diversity, and we may come to see why Henry I chose to build his great monastery, his mausoleum, in Reading.

TIMELINES

Geological periods referred to in the text

Cretaceous 100-65 million years ago (Earth's age 4.5billion years approx.)	Quaternary 2.6 million years ago to present

Human Settlement Period A

Pre-history in Britain

The Stone Age			Bronze Age	Iron Age
Palaeolithic	**Mesolithic**	**Neolithic**	**2500-800 BC**	**800 BC-43 AD**
Pre 12,000 BC	**12,000-4,000 BC**	**4,000-2,500 BC**	Expansion of permanent settlements, development of large-scale field systems. Monuments such as round barrows and production of metalwork (bronze).	Social and technological change with development of iron working and hillforts. Calleva founded. Roman Conquest.
The main evidence for this period comes from flint tools, including hand axes.	Hunter-gatherers. Evidence consists mainly of worked flint and microliths	Deforestation and agriculture established. Monumental stone structures (e.g. Stonehenge) long barrows and pottery appear.		

Human Settlement Period B

43 to 1154 AD

This era is marked by an increase in written historical records

Roman Berkshire 43 AD - early 5th century	Anglo-Saxon Berkshire Early 5th century - 870s	Saxon - Danish Berkshire 870s - 1066	Norman England 1066 -1154
Building of villas and roads. Calleva was expanded and became known as Calleva Atrebatum (Silchester). There is evidence of thriving Romano-British farming settlements and of continuing Iron Age culture. Most of the evidence is archaeological rather than written.	Arrival of Germanic tribes (Angles and Saxons), replacing the Romano-British culture, followed by the spread of Christianity. Evidence is based on several manuscripts such as Bede's *Ecclesiastical History of the English People.* But much of the evidence is still archaeological, such as pottery and the remnants of other artefacts. The name of 'Reading' appears for the first time.	The Viking invasions of the north spread to southern England. Known as the Danish army, the invaders were non-Christian. Following the victories of Alfred the Great in the 870s and 880s, there was continual sporadic warfare between the Saxons and the Danes until the beginning of the 10th century. Sources include various writings such as the Anglo-Saxon Chronicle as well as archaeology.	The Conquest of England by Duke William of Normandy not only changed the socio-political structure of the country but brought about many more reliable written records, such as the Domesday Book of 1086. Much of the evidence for Reading remains archaeological rather than written. 1121, King Henry I founded a monastery in Reading. This established the outline of the modern town. In 1154 Henry II, the first of the Plantagenet dynasty, was crowned.

MAP OF READING

The following map shows Reading and Caversham, together with the confluence of the River Thames with the River Kennet. Although the book will look at areas further afield, it is this area, within the marked oval, that is the focus of attention. We will see when, why, and how, Reading replaced Calleva, (Silchester), as the main town of the area.

MAP C

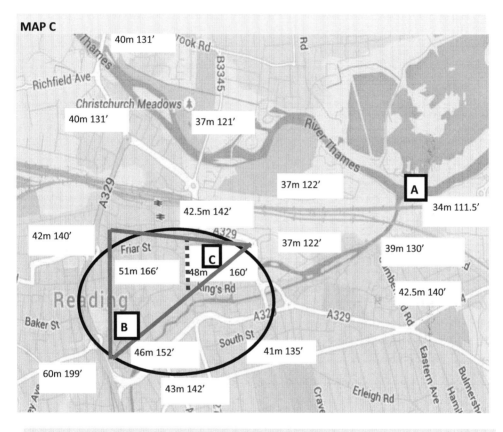

Map of Reading with heights above sea level in metres and feet. The oval line shows an approximate indication of the area suitable for human settlement. The triangle gives the best lines of defence. The dotted line shows the westerly extent of today's Abbey Quarter and coincides with the possible line of defence at the time of the Danish Viking invasion in 870-871. The heights given are OD (Ordnance Datum) levels in metres (m) and feet (').

A.   Confluence of the rivers Thames and Kennet.

B.   St Mary's Minster.

C.   The Forbury and site of Reading monastery and Abbey, (1121-1539).

READING: ITS TOPOGRAPHY AND EARLY SETTLEMENTS

The confluence of the rivers Thames and Kennet makes an ideal location for a settlement. To the east there are naturally occurring aids to defence. There is the marshy land around the area where the two rivers meet. Likewise, on the north bank of the easterly approaches of the Thames, low-lying marshy ground creates a natural barrier. Upstream, and moving west, after the rivers separate, the Thames hugs the rising contours of Caversham, leaving a large expanse of more marshy ground on its south bank. In the fork formed between the Kennet and the Thames, the land rises sharply, but then falls equally quickly to the river Kennet and the other streams that flow from the west and the south. The ground again rises along the south bank of the Kennet. It is this central wedge-shaped triangle which gives Reading its distinctive appearance.

This 1840s illustration of the early Great Western Railway shows the terrain from Kennet Mouth looking west.[1] This is a marshy land criss-crossed with streams leading to and from the Kennet and Thames. The church of St James, newly built in 1840, is the first visible building.[2] It is clearly standing on elevated land. After the 1120s, until its destruction 400 years later, the Abbey's great tower, with its gleaming white limestone, more than 40 metres high, would have been the traveller's first sight as he approached the town.

In addition to the rivers Thames and Kennet, there are several other cuts and rivulets which likewise protect the town. No doubt some of these, such as the Holy Brook and the Plummery stream, were enhanced, or even created, by human hand over the passage of time.[3] Nevertheless, this does not detract from the protective role they played in securing Reading's defences.

---

1. Marked A on the map, page 3
2. Marked X on the illustration on this page. (Illustration courtesy of Reading Library)
3. *UO* p 263, Sub-title *Water Supply*

Allowing for particular variations, the overall geology of the area is one of alluvial silt over gravel on top of chalk.[1] This combination is ideal for human settlement, being conducive to small-scale food production, building and the provision of fresh water supplies. Water is one of the necessities for life. As such, the rivers provided this vital resource. We also know that in the Forbury, it was possible to tap down to fresh water. As late as the 19th century, maps show the existence of a well where the cloisters of the 1121 monastery stood.[2] Other maps indicate that at least one spring may have risen in the western section of what is now the Forbury Gardens, and flowed down to the Thames.

Bedrock Geology

LONDON CLAY FORMATION: CLAY, SILT AND SAND

LAMBETH GROUP: CLAY, SILT AND SAND

SEAFORD AND NEWHAVEN CHALK FORMATION

The bedrock of the Reading area is Seaford Formation and Newhaven Chalk Formation, (undifferentiated). This is a sedimentary bedrock formed approximately between 100 to 65 million years ago, in the Upper Cretaceous Period, in an environment dominated by warm chalk seas.

The rocks were formed in warm shallow 'chalk shelf' seas. They often consist of calcareous ooze of microscopic remains of plankton, especially disc-shaped calcite shapes or coccoliths that make up spherical coccolithphores. These latter are spherical cells about 5–100 micrometres across, enclosed by calcareous plates called coccoliths, which are about 2–25 micrometres across.

The Superficial Geology, over the bedrock. This occurred up to two and half million years ago during the Quaternary Period.

These top layers were formed from rivers depositing mainly sand and gravel (detrital) material in channels to form river terrace deposits. Together with fine silt and clay from flooding, these create floodplain alluvium.

1. The gravel layer, with variations, is approximately 14′ (4.3m) deep
2. For example see the Ordnance Survey map of 1879.

Introduction

Although Reading may be said to be a town on the Kennet, rather than on the Thames, it was the latter that provided the settlement, and later the town, with its principal means of communication by water, via Wallingford and Oxford to the north and north-west, and so to the centre of England, and to London to the east. The Kennet Valley also opened up a transport route to the rich agricultural uplands to the west of Reading, with its wool-producing area, as well as providing a direct link to Newbury in the west, and access to the south.

The town's more westerly section, which rises significantly above the surrounding country, is served by several rivers and streams, and is close to an ideal place for crossing the Thames. This latter is an important consideration. Necessary as it was to secure a defensible position, any settlement, or town, also needs trade links. To the east of Reading, owing to the marshy terrain, there are no natural crossing places of the Thames for some miles. Opposite Reading, where Caversham now lies, there is an ideal location for such a crossing before the hills rise to form a barrier as one moves westwards towards Mapledurham, until reaching Goring. Here the Goring Gap allows another crossing point, as used by the creators of the Ridgeway path. Although the approaches to the Thames on Reading's south bank of the Thames are marshy, they are sufficiently elevated to allow access to a crossing point at Caversham.

There has been a long-standing debate as to the exact location of the first settlement in the area, and so the beginnings of Reading. The map on page three shows that the contours, as indicated by land-height, favour anywhere in the section enclosed within the heavy oval line. The focus of attention, though, must be the 'golden triangle'. This demonstrates the locational advantage of higher defensible land, but also shows how the further west the settlement boundary moves, despite being at a higher elevation, the width of the area requiring man-made defences increases. To some extent, early settlers would be presented with the dilemma of occupying, and utilising, the advantages of a greater area of higher land, against the disadvantages of having a much broader front to defend.

Bearing this in mind, it has been proposed that the area around St Mary's Minster is the most likely site of the earliest Saxon settlement. It is also on the way to any road to the south, and in a direct line with the crossing to Caversham in the north.[1] The other possibility is the more defensible easterly area, now occupied by the Forbury, with its more elevated contours, and its freshwater well, or wells, which would have provided a secure base for settlement.[2]

---

1. *UO,* and marked 'B' on the map, page 3.
2. Marked 'C' on the map, page 3.

THE ARCHAEOLOGY

An Overview

We see from the topography that the land between the rivers Thames and Kennet provided an ideal area for human habitation. This is confirmed by the archaeology.[1] There is sufficient evidence from the mid to late Bronze Age (c. 1000 BC), to suggest continual and intensive settlement over this period. Lobb and Rose claim that the number of Iron Age coins dating to the first century BC, especially at the confluence of the Thames and Kennet, is indicative of the importance of the area.[2] As noted, the nature of settlement before, and even during, the Roman period, remains unclear. We shall see that there is evidence of farmsteads, and maybe even of a villa, on the Caversham side of the Thames, possibly with Christian connections.[3] This would lead one to speculate that there was a river crossing at this point, leading to Calleva Atrebatum (Silchester) to the south, and today's Oxford area in the north.[4]

The withdrawal of Roman imperial forces in the early 5th century led to the turmoil which dominated these islands for the remainder of the millennium. It has been pointed out that the evidence for early Saxon settlement is archaeological, rather than through written historical records. There is even archaeological evidence that Germanic forces were in the area before the final Roman withdrawal. One such example is the burial at Dyke Hills, near Dorchester, of a Germanic soldier and of a woman with a cruciform brooch.[5] Early 5th century pottery has also been discovered on both banks of the Thames and there is an unbroken pottery and metalwork record from the early 4th to the 5th century. All this evidence is confirmed by the existence of cemeteries belonging to communities probably based on military and/or farming settlements. There is some evidence that these encampments radiated from the bridgehead at Dorchester. These were possibly a northernmost line of defence along the Thames, and formed a territorial demarcation for a major settlement at Silchester which continued even after the departure of the Roman imperial army.[6]

In Reading itself, much of the evidence of possible Roman occupation lies under later developments. Nevertheless, Saxon pottery and metalwork have been

---

1. *UO* Ch 1.

2. Lobb S and Rose P *Archaeological survey of the lower Kennet Valley.* Wessex Archaeological Report 9. 1996.

3. Reading Museum has a font with the Christian XP (Chi Rho = Christos) emblem discovered at Dean's Farm. See page 38, note 3)

4. Salway P *Roman Oxfordshire.*

5. Yorke B *Wessex in the Early Middle Ages* p812

6. Myers J *Anglo-Saxon Pottery and the Settlement of England* pp 70-85

uncovered in several sites. For instance, in the 1970s, Slade's excavations of the Norman Abbey uncovered early to mid-Saxon (c.400 AD-850 AD) pottery and metalwork.[1]

The extensive archaeological excavation of the Oracle site again revealed pottery of the same period. No structural remains were identified in the environs of St Mary's Minster church, although several scholars believe this area is where the earliest Saxon town stood. Among other evidence of occupation and settlement are numerous artefacts, such as the Viking sword uncovered in the 1830s. Reading Museum also holds the Thames Water Collection. These finds are the result of dredging the non-tidal section of the river from its source to Teddington.

Current archaeological evidence, from the Saxon to Norman periods, can best be summarised as having two foci. The first of these lies in the eastern section of the town, in what has become known as the Abbey Quarter. This area had been the subject of illustrations and sporadic excavations since the middle of the 18th century. This was due partly to the growing interest, from the mid-18th century, in the Norman Abbey, and partly because, unlike much of the rest of Reading, the site had not been almost completely covered over by later buildings and roads. In fact, whenever excavations are undertaken in this area, samples of Saxon habitation come to light. These range from sherds of pottery, and metal objects, to skeletons and even evidence of buildings predating the 1121 monastery. For example, one of the best recorded excavations, as noted above, was carried out by Cecil Slade in the 1970s. Slade lists the Saxon artefacts uncovered in the apse section of the chancel of the 1121 monastery. His account also includes a photograph which shows what he describes as *the pre-Abbey footings under the Abbey footings.*[2]

As already seen, extensive archaeological investigations were carried out by Oxford Archaeology, between 1996 and 1998, on the second site, namely around the Oracle. The results are to be found in the book *Under the Oracle*.

Through the course of this work we shall be examining in greater detail the various excavations and historical records alluded to above. We shall also look at, and examine, the various theories that they have generated. The aim is to give the reader an overview of how Reading developed, to demonstrate what role it played in the wider story of British/English history, and perhaps even to offer a deeper insight into why it was here that one of the country's greatest religious foundations, Reading's monastery, later to become an Abbey, was founded in 1121.

---

1. Slade, C. *Excavation at Reading Abbey 1971-1973* BAJ Vol 68 pages 61 and 65

2. ibid p 38. On page 31, of his work, Slade describes the soil types and details of this area of the excavation.

CHAPTER 1

THE FIRST SETTLEMENTS

THE STONE AGE - BRONZE AGE - EARLY IRON AGE

The Stone Age

The Palaeolithic, Mesolithic and Neolithic periods

There is evidence of early pre-Roman settlement in the Reading area, but it is sporadic and inconclusive. As we have seen, the topography suggests a desirable location, and there is sufficient archaeology to validate the hypothesis of continuing occupation over a long period. There is more doubt about the degree of concentration and density of population. Evidence for habitation in and around Reading can be found from Palaeolithic times onward, although it is not until the Mesolithic period that river lines and levels approximated to those of today.

Among the finds to the north of the river there have been copious examples of hand axes and choppers in the gravel deposits around Emmer Green.[1] There is also an abundance of material to support the theory of continuous Mesolithic and Neolithic human activity all along the Thames Valley.

Emmer Green, Palaeolithic hand axe

Few, if any, prehistoric sites have been identified within the area of the medieval borough. In all probability, this is the consequence of subsequent building and development, resulting in the destruction of prehistoric evidence and impeding excavation. Surrounding terrain, similar to that within Reading, has given sufficient evidence of Stone Age activity to support this view. As noted, this holds true especially for the Mesolithic and Neolithic periods.

Neolithic saddle quern. Grain is placed in the 'saddle' and ground down to make flour by rubbing the upper stone over it.

The arrival of more technically advanced peoples, around 3000 BC, ushered in marked changes in land-use in the Reading area. These peoples brought with

---

1. *Emmer Green Past and Present, p22.* Emmer Green Residents' Association 2001.

them pottery, quern stones, arable farming, animal husbandry and, of course, the culture that created Stonehenge.[1]

There is some debate concerning the amount of land used for arable, as opposed to livestock, farming, at this time. It has been suggested that much of the cereal crop was grown as fodder for livestock, and for making beer. This is based on bone analysis which suggests that the diet of Neolithic people consisted of little that was not of animal origin. Whether this is the case, or not, there can be little doubt that it was during this period that, in the south of Britain, much of the virgin forest was cleared, especially on the easily-worked Upper Thames gravels. Subsequently the chalk downlands were settled by herdsmen, whilst the easily-worked floodplain, consisting of alluvium, sand and gravel, was used for mixed farming.

Grooved Ware,
Late Neolithic, Melbourne, Scotland [3]

Along with improvements in agricultural techniques, the Neolithic peoples brought with them art and decorated pottery. It should be remembered that we are dealing with a very wide range of dates of about 2000 years, from c.4000 to c.2500 BC. Consequently, techniques changed and developed over this time.

The evidence left by these people, such as Stonehenge and the Windmill Hill causewayed enclosure near Avebury, testifies to their long-lasting influence on the landscape, one that was to carry on through the ages, even to the present day.

This also holds true for the Middle Thames, as shown by the existence of a similar causewayed enclosure discovered in Abingdon.[2] In both these cases, and in others throughout the south of England, the archaeological evidence from pottery is consistent with a widespread culture throughout the area. It is reasonable, therefore, to assume its existence in Reading.

---

1. Stonehenge Visitor Centre. English Heritage display of Neolithic life

2. Other similar Neolithic sites are Whitehawk Camp, The Trundle (W. Sussex), Hambledon Hill, Hembury, Coombe Hill, Rams Hill (Berkshire Downs) and Crickley Hill (Cheltenham). Even as this was being written a new causewayed enclosure was being excavated by *Oxford Archaeology* at Thame.

3. (Insert) Courtesy of *Biggar Archaeological Group. (BAG)* For more information about this dig see their web site http://www.biggararchaeology.org.uk/pdf_reports/BAG_MELBOURNE.pdf. This discovery near Glasgow shows how widely, throughout the British Isles, these techniques had spread by the late Neolithic period. A similar artefact was discovered in Caversham, but free illustrations are not available. My special thanks to BAG.

Evidence for settlement in the Bronze and Iron Ages

Before looking in more detail at the development pattern of settlements in Reading, we should make a distinction between the Middle and the Upper Thames Valley. Reading lies in the Middle Thames section and the evidence points to differences in settlement between the two areas.

The easily-worked gravel of the Thames Valley, namely the calcareous and neutral soils of the flat well-drained gravel terraces, proved as attractive as the chalk and limestone hills.[1] Moreover, the rising water levels also facilitated waterborne communications and human settlement, following as they did the linear pattern, not just of the Thames, but of its tributaries. Whereas evidence in the Bronze Age is sketchy, the same pattern is clearly demonstrated by Iron Age enclosures such as those found in Thames Valley Park, east of Reading.

By the late Iron Age, there was a move away from the low-lying gravel areas, as testified by the development of Calleva (Silchester). The rising water table and deposits of sedimentary alluvium indicate a shift in settlement patterns during the Iron Age. In Reading, at Green Park, there is evidence of cultivation of grass for grazing, along with pollen samples indicating the cultivation of other crops.

The above factors lead to the conclusion that the Middle Thames was not as 'settled' as the Upper Thames, namely from Wallingford to Oxford, and even beyond. Nevertheless, the Middle Thames was being cleared for grazing grassland, with some crops, though with less arable farming than in the upper reaches of the valley. The lower Kennet Valley, especially at its confluence with the Thames, seems to have been a centre of agricultural activity. Even as far upstream as Aldermarston Wharf, there is evidence of the cultivation and storage of emmer and high protein six-row barley.

It is only in the Roman period, 2nd century AD, that we find evidence for hay making.[2] However, the discovery of a scythe-like tool dating to the late Iron Age may mean that this technique of storing feed for cattle predates the Roman era.

What this all demonstrates is the developing, and shifting, patterns of human settlement and how they are related, at least in part, to the changes in geological and meteorological factors. What is certain, as we shall see, is that Reading and its hinterland reflected the overall development of settlement.

1. *The Thames Through Time, The Archaeology of the Gravel Terraces of the Upper and Middle Thames: The Early Historical Period: AD1-1000.* Booth et al. Oxford Archaeology 2007. To a large extent, it is evidence for settlement in the Bronze and Iron Ages from the findings quoted in this report, that has been used in this book .
2. Miles, D, Palmer, S, Smith, A and Jones, G *Iron Age and Roman settlement in the Upper Thames Valley: Excavations at Claydon Pike and other sites within the Cotswold Water Park.* Thames Valley Landscapes Monograph, Oxford Archaeology, Claydon Pike.

Bronze and Iron Age Settlement In The Reading Area

MAP A

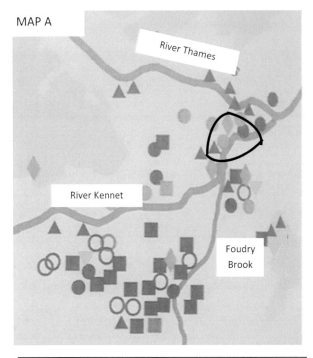

Map A. Human activity in and around Reading from the Bronze Age through to Roman Britain.

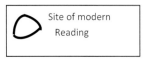

	Site of modern Reading

BRONZE AGE

▽ Barrow/ring ditch

▲ Metalwork

● Other finds

○ Cremation/burials

■ Site

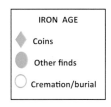

IRON AGE

◆ Coins

● Other finds

○ Cremation/burial

MAP B

Human expansion and exploitation of the Thames Valley.

MAP B

Extensive forest

Increasing Clearance

Wet woodland

c1400BC

Little runoff

Low permanent water table
NO FLOODING

Mixed farming

Clearance for rough pasture

Mixed farming

Specialist grazing

c1400-150BC

Increased runoff but no erosion

Rising permanent water table
FLOODING

Increased arable

More intensive landuse

Mixed farming

Intensive Grazing

150BC-400AD

Increased runoff plus erosion

High permanent water table
FLOODING and ALLUVIATION

Source for this page: *The Thames through Time.* Oxford Archaeology

The Bronze Age, 2500-800 BC

The progression from stone to metal-worked implements was gradual, and varied according to geographical location. The peoples who settled in Britain during the second and third millennia BC were part of a global industrial revolution. Geographically, the history of metal working can be traced as far afield as China and the Middle East, as well as western Europe. Theories regarding the timescale have changed. Some scholars now believe that, far from originating at one point, and spreading outwards, the discovery of how to smelt an ore, so as to extract its metal, occurred independently in several places.

Initially, because of its plentiful supply and its ease of use, copper became the metal of choice. As such, much early metallurgy consisted solely of copper-smelted goods. There is evidence of copper smelting from c. 4000 BC. This era is sometimes referred to as the Chalcolithic period, (from the Greek *chalco* meaning copper and *lithos* meaning stone), to indicate the overlap between the first use of metal and the continued use of stone.

It is necessary to be careful about the definition of 'bronze'. The process of smelting copper with a variety of other compounds, to create an alloy, varied at different times and in different places. In some cases arsenic was the additive of choice, though the most commonly accepted definition of bronze is that it is an alloy of copper with about 12% tin. The abundance of tin in parts of Britain, and specifically its availability with copper, as in Cornwall, certainly facilitated the spread of bronze in this region.

Geneticists and archaeologists have long debated the origins of the peoples who occupied Britain, and indeed Europe, in the Stone and Bronze Ages. In recent times several DNA studies have been used to propose various theories.[1] Whatever the relationship between the groups, or how one may have replaced the other, there is ample evidence around Reading, as shown on the charts opposite, of large-scale Bronze Age settlement.

In the early 1900s, artefacts from a Bronze Age barrow were discovered in south Reading, in the area of Cressingham Road and Northcourt Avenue.[2] To the north, in Caversham, sherds of Bronze Age pottery are listed by Reading

---

1. For instance, in June 2015 *Nature* reported the results of two independent researches from the Universities of Harvard and Copenhagen, which suggested that there were three waves of separate DNA types in western Europe. The earliest dated back to over 9000 years ago, with another arriving about 7000 years ago and a final group arriving about 4000 years ago. If David Reich, of Harvard Medical School, is correct then it was, as he writes, *an amazing cultural process where you have groups which are as genetically distinct as Europeans and East Asians but living side by side for thousands of years.* See Appendix B , page 119
2. Seaby, W. *Some Pre-Roman Remains from South Reading.* BAJ 36

Museum as coming from Emmer Green. Three socketed Bronze Age axes were discovered when Emmer Green Primary School was being built in 1951. These are dated as belonging to the late Bronze Age (1000-700 BC). There are several other examples of Bronze Age settlement in the area, such as those reported in 1979/80 at Burghfield.[1]

It is likely that during this period, all along the Thames Valley, villages of round huts were being built. These would have been surrounded by ring ditches, and round barrows would have been constructed for the burial of the dead. The Thames was an important trading route, with settlements along its length. There is evidence of contact with the Mediterranean, Egypt and the Baltic, with finds of amber and gold.[2]

A comb-decorated Bronze Age beaker sherd from Carwood Farm, Scotland.[4]

Also on the gravel to the north of the Kennet, at Southcote, there lies a possible Bronze Age barrow where an early Iron Age site was identified, but it remains largely unexcavated.[3]

Pottery, weapons, brooches, and other remains of these times, are found in quantity along the Thames Valley, including Reading.

The progression from Bronze Age to Iron Age was gradual, with a considerable degree of overlap. In Europe it is usual to identify three main waves of Iron Age settlement, known as Hallstatt, La Tène and Belgic: the latter being associated with the north-west of Europe, including Britain. The first of these is named after Hallstatt in Austria where, in the mid 19th century, a distinctive type of metal-working culture was identified.[5] This civilisation, beginning around 1200 BC, is itself divided by archaeologists into four main categories, as it evolved into the more technologically advanced Iron Age culture known as La Tène. The latter is named after the archaeological site in Switzerland on the northern side of Lake Neuchâtel. This has been dated to about 500 BC. Archaeology from all these periods has been found in the Thames Valley and in Reading.

1. Bradley, R and Richards, J. *Excavation of Two Ring Ditches at Heron's House, Burghfield.* BAJ 70

2. Wilson, David Gordon. *The Making of the Middle Thames* p26.

3. Seaby, W A. *Some Pre-Roman Remains from South Reading.* BAJ 36

4. Courtesy of *Biggar Archaeological Group. (BAG)* See note 3 page 10. Similar items have been found in the Reading area. BAG kindly allowed me free use of their images. Local sources would not permit free usage.

5. Hallstatt A-B are part of the Bronze Age culture, dating to c.1200-750 BC whereas Hallstatt C-D are Iron Age.

The Iron Age , 800 BC - 43 AD

The introduction of iron, and the use of iron-shod ploughs, allowed for the expansion of agriculture on the uplands around Reading. The Celtic-Belgic tribes were now able to go beyond the easily worked gravel and sandy soils of the low-lying levels, and cultivate the heavier soils of the hill tops and slopes. [1]

The riverside gravels still maintained the most productive farms. There was probably an element of over-cropping and soil exhaustion, and there is evidence that the inhabitants moved up and down the valley, leaving areas fallow for some years to recuperate. The archaeology also shows a certain permanence, with carefully cared-for pottery and lavishly decorated personal domestic articles and weapons. The type of round barrow in the Mortimer area, only a mile or so from Silchester, indicates early Iron Age settlement.

The Thames Valley and Silchester

The first wave of Belgic-Celt invaders appeared in the Thames Valley towards the end of the 2nd century BC. According to Boon, the numismatic record indicates that Calleva, (Silchester), was known to them. If so, and this may apply to earlier settlers, it may be that it was its remoteness that attracted them. We know that the Thames, at Reading as elsewhere, acted both as a barrier and a frontier.[2] We shall see more of this when looking at the territories of two of these tribes, the Catuvellauni and the Atrebates, in the next section.

There is no shortage of archaeology for these periods in the whole of the Thames Valley, and near Reading. For instance, there is the evidence of late Iron Age occupation at Knowle Hill [3] and from the extensive finds at Aldermaston Wharf, just to the west of Reading. These span a time-frame reaching from the late Bronze Age though to the middle Iron Age.[4]

---

1. There appear to have been two waves of Celtic invasion. The first, during the 4th century BC, spread quickly to Ireland and later to the Isle of Man and Scotland. Their language and culture developed into what we today know as Gaelic or Goidelic. Linguistically this language is referred to as Q Celtic as it retained the 'q' or 'kw' sound. The second wave into southern Britain and Wales is today referred to as Brythonic or Brittonic. This is known as P Celtic as it adopted the P sound. An example of this is the word for 'son of'. In Goidelic this is *Mac* or *Mc* (note the final 'q' or 'kw' sound) whereas in Welsh it was *Map* which was abbreviated to *Ap*. (See also Crystal, D. *The Cambridge Encyclopaedia of Language*).   We will be examining the debate concerning the ethnicity of these peoples later.

2. Boon, G.C. *Silchester, The Roman Town of Calleva*, 1974

3. Over, L. *A Belgic occupation site at Knowle Hill, Berks.* BAJ 67

4. Cowell, R.W. Fulford, M.G. & Lobb, S. *Excavations of Prehistoric and Roman Settlements at Aldermaston Wharf.* BAJ 69

Chapter 1

The archaeological evidence demonstrates that there were several settlement sites along the Thames in the region of Reading.

As Boon says:

> when circumstances favoured the creation of a larger settlement ... the Silchester spur was chosen because it was the most southerly and therefore one to be secured against seizure by hostile forces who might overrun the rest of the plateau.[1]

For this reason the confluence of the Kennet and Thames was not chosen as the main settlement. Indeed, it appears likely that it was a strategic frontier point and, judging by the known situation immediately before Caesar's invasion, under constant threat from north of the River.

We referred above to the Belgic Celts. In the next section we shall be looking at these peoples in more detail, and will examine the theory that they may not even have been Celts. Whatever their ethnicity, they would have been among the earliest inhabitants of the area that today we call Reading.

---

1. Boon, *ibid p 37*

CHAPTER 2

PRE-ROMAN SETTLEMENTS

The General Background

There is well documented archaeological and historical evidence for the period immediately preceding the Romanisation of Britain.[1]

By the end of the first century BC, Calleva, (Silchester), had been established as a major town of the Atrebates, a Celtic, or Belgic, group, whose name appears both in Gaul and Britain.

First, we shall examine the evidence for this pre-Roman settlement, and some of the opinions derived from it.

It is Reading's association with Calleva, and the territory that it commanded, that has relevance to the origins of the town. We shall see later, when looking at the toponomy of the name of Reading, just how important this may be.

Caesar famously begins his *Commentary on the Gallic War* with the words: *All Gaul is divided into three parts, one of which the Belgae inhabit, another the Aquitani, a third is inhabited by those who in their own language are called Celts, but in ours Gauls.*[2] The next sentence, *All these differ from each other in language, customs and laws,*[3] is the one which provokes academic debate and has implications later in our search for the origins of the naming of the town of Reading. To understand Caesar it is helpful to examine a map of Gaul as he described it.[4]

---

1. Latin texts, such as Caesar's *Commentarii de Bello Gallico*, (DBG), give us detailed accounts from the Roman viewpoint. The Winchester Hoard is a prime example of archaeological evidence. Cf. *Hampshire Field Club & Archaeological Society, Newsletter 43 - Spring 2005.*

2. DBG 1, 1 *Gallia est omnis divisa in partes tres, quarum unam incolunt Belgae, aliam Aquitani, tertiam qui ipsorum lingua Celtae, nostra Galli appellantur.*

3. DBG 1, 1. *Hi omnes lingua, institutis, legibus inter se differunt.*

4. The boundaries shown on the map are approximate; different historians give slightly different borders, but the overall picture is a good representation of how Caesar saw the divisions within Gaul.

Portus Itius

The lands of the Atrebates tribe lay to the south of Portus Itius, as marked on the map.

Though presumed to be near modern Calais or Boulogne, the port's exact location is unknown. Caesar refers to it twice with a meaning that may be a version of 'Port of Departure'.[1]

What is fairly certain is that the main city of the Atrebates was Nemetocenna (also known as Nemetacum), which became Nemetocenna Atrebatum. It has been suggested that this later gave rise to its modern name of Arras.

Nemetocenna is named after the Celtic goddess of sacred groves, Nemetona. Throughout Britain there were groves associated with water dedicated to Arnemetia (Celtic *are* - 'beside' and *nemeton* - 'goddess of the grove'). Celtic druids have became famous, or maybe infamous, following Tacitus' description of the sacred groves on the island of Mona (Anglesey) at the time of the Boudiccan insurrection.[2] Although these reports were biased, to justify the undoubted brutal suppression by the Romans of their Celtic enemies, few doubt a certain degree of truth concerning the rituals.

Because of its later appearance in Britain, when the appendage *Atrebatum,* ('of the Atrebates'), was added to Calleva, it is important to understand how this tribe, based in modern northern France, came to play such an important role in the Reading area. The name, *Atrebas,* itself has given rise to several theories about its origins.

One etymological explanation is that the name has Celtic roots derived from the word *treb* (Irish 'farm' or 'building', Welsh *tref,* 'house', Middle Breton *treff,*

---

1. DBG 5. 2 *Collaudatis militibus atque eis qui negotio praefuerant, quid fieri velit ostendit atque omnes ad* **portum Itium** *convenire iubet* . (Having commended the soldiers and those who had presided over the work, he informs them what he wishes to be done, and orders all the ships to assemble at the **Port of Itius**)

2. 60 AD. Tacitus *Annals XIV 30* . *Nam cruore captivo adolere aras et hominum fibris consulere deos fas habebant.* ("They consulted their deities through human entrails and believed it a divine duty to cover their altars with captives' blood.") Lucan in *Pharsalia* describes one such grove at Marseilles: *Altars stood in its midst with the images of the gods. Every tree was stained with sacrificial blood.*

'city'). Another explanation is that it comes from the Celtic for inland dwellers, in contrast to the sea-coast dwelling Belgic tribe along this section of the coast, who are referred to by Caesar as the 'Morini'. Some scholars believe this is a reference to their maritime location.[1]

Before looking at the connection between the British and Belgic Atrebates it is necessary to clarify the terminology used by Caesar and by historians today. We have seen how Caesar claims that the inhabitants of the three parts of Gaul had different languages. Caesar states that the Belgic tribes had Germanic, or Teutonic origins. This has been, and continues to be, the cause of dispute, namely as to whether the Belgic tribes, and so their language, were in fact not Celtic.[2] Comment appears to focus on the Belgic element and little on the Aquitani. Yet if, as Caesar claims, all three were different, one from another, then this should equally hold true of the Aquitani, in south west Gaul.

Those who favour the argument that the Belgic tribes were not Celts, claim that these peoples possessed a proto-Teutonic language, as evidenced by the relative lack of Celtic place names in the areas of Britain occupied by these tribes. Contrary to this, and by far the greatest body of opinion, is that the Celtic group, including those who came from the area we call Germany today, belonged to the same linguistic grouping. This, therefore, includes both the Belgae and Aquitani.

The importance to our studies is that, if we accept this hypothesis, the Atrebates were a Celtic people, speaking a Celtic language. Such a conclusion, as we shall see later, has significant implications when considering the etymological origins of the word *Reading*, let alone the genetic make-up of its population.[2]

The Link between Britain and Gaul

Thanks to Caesar we have a detailed description of the man who led the Atrebates in Gaul, of how he came to rule in Britain, and of the dynasty he founded, with its connections to Calleva, or Silchester as we know it today.

In Caesar's accounts, the Latinised version of his name is Commius. Caesar recounts how he appointed Commius to be king of the Belgic Atrebates after he, Caesar, had defeated and subdued them. Caesar also states how much he trusted his new ally. Commius was rewarded not just by being made king, with his capital at Nemetocenna, but he was excused taxes and was granted the lands of the neighbouring Morini.

---

1. *Mor* being similar to *Mar*, Latin for *sea*. Wightman, Edith Mary (1985), *Gallia Belgica*, University of California Press, page 29.

2. For an example of this debate see works by Geoffrey Sampson and Lary Trask on one hand and Stephen Oppenheimer, in his book *The Origins of the British* (2006), on the other. David Crystal is firmly of the opinion that they all belong to the Celtic family. (*Cambridge Encyclopaedia of Language*. p304).

Commius further distinguished himself during Caesar's campaign in Britain.[1] At a crucial point, he came to Caesar's aid with thirty cavalrymen, whom he had brought over from Gaul.[2] When, in 54 BC, Caesar defeated the British leader Cassivellaunus it was Commius who negotiated the peace terms between him and Caesar.[3]

However, the alliance and friendship between Commius and Caesar ended when Caesar's deputy in Gaul, the legate, Titus Labienus, believing that Commius was playing a double game, enticed Commius and his followers to a meeting where he attacked and tried to kill them. Commius escaped, but at this point he most certainly did become an enemy of Rome. It was said that Commius made a resolution never again *to come within sight of any Roman*.[4]

Commius, shortly afterwards, gathered his forces to come to the relief of the besieged Celts, commanded by Vercingetorix, in the hill fort of Alesia.[5]

Despite Caesar's victory at Alesia in 52 BC, Commius once again managed to escape, and apparently returned north to his Atrebatic lands. Caesar went in pursuit and took the Atrebatic capital of Nemetocenna. Commius continued a guerrilla-type warfare by *supporting himself and his adherents on plunder by means of his cavalry; he infested the roads, and intercepted several convoys which were bringing provisions to the Roman winter quarters.*[6]

The final engagement came when Commius encountered the Roman cavalry commander, Caius Volusenus Quadratus. After a short engagement, with losses on both sides, Volusenus' superior, Antonius (Mark Antony), agreed to accept hostages from Commius, who promised to go wherever Antonius prescribed. It would appear from this account that Commius left for Britain at this point.

A different version appears in Sextus Julius Frontinus's *Strategemata*. Here we read that *Commius, the Atrebatean, when defeated by the deified Julius, fled from Gaul to Britain, and happened to reach the Channel at a time when the*

---

1. DBG 4, 21 *Commium, quem ipse Atrebatibus superatis regem ibi constituerat, cuius et virtutem et consilium probabat et quem sibi fidelem esse arbitrabatur cuiusque auctoritas in his regionibus magni habebatur, mittit.* (Commius, whom, upon subduing the Atrebates, he had created king there, a man whose courage and conduct he esteemed and who he thought would be faithful to him, and whose influence ranked highly in those countries). The spelling appears variously as Commios, Comius, Comnios
2. DBG 4,35 *equites ..., quos Commius Atrebas, secum transportaverat,* (cavalrymen ... whom Commius the Atrebean and brought with him). The use of the verb *transportare* (to transport) suggests that these had been brought from Gaul and not from the British Atrebatic tribal lands.
3. DBG 5, 22
4. DBG 8, 23 *dicebatur numquam in conspectum cuiusquam Romani venire.* (Book 8 was completed by Aulus Hirtius after Caesar's death).
5. Alesia lies north-west of Dijon in Burgundy. The siege and battle were in 52BC
6. DBG 8, 47 *cum suis equitibus latrociniis se suos que alebat infestisque itineribus commeatus complures, qui comportabantur in hiberna Romanorum, intercipiebat.*

wind was fair, but the tide was out. Although the vessels were stranded on the flats, he nevertheless ordered the sails to be spread. Caesar, who was following them from a distance, seeing the sails swelling with the full breeze, and imagining Commius to be escaping from his hands and to be proceeding on a prosperous voyage, abandoned the pursuit.[1]

Commius and the Atrebates in Britain

We saw above that Commius had accompanied Caesar to Britain in his campaign against Cassivellanus and the Catuvellauni tribe with their allies, in 54 BC. There is some uncertainty about how and why Commius later returned to Britain. As noted, there are two versions offered, one in the *Strategemata* and another in *De bello Gallico.*

One interpretation is that Commius was in fact sent by Caesar to Britain and installed as a king well-disposed to the Romans. Certainly the involvement by Commius in the defeat of Cassivellaunus, meant that he may well have received the support of the British tribes opposed to the expansion of the Catuvellauni.

This apparent rapprochement between Caesar and Commius might also be explained by the defection of Labienus to Pompey in the Roman Civil War of 49-45 BC.

It had been Labienus who first accused Commius of treachery and who had attacked him and his companions, leading to Commius' support for Vercingetorix at the siege of Alesia. It was the attack by Labienus which Commius claimed had turned him against the Romans. Consequently, it has been argued, Labienus' support of the anti-Caesarean popularist party in the Roman Civil War resulted in Caesar turning once again to his erstwhile Gallic ally, Commius.

The whole Commius narrative has been brought into question by pointing out that the main sources are hardly unbiased. Hirtius, who completed Caesar's *Gallic Wars*, was Governor of Transalpine Gaul and was involved in the Roman Civil War towards the end of Caesars's life and after Caesar's murder. Although a contemporary, he had his own agenda.

Frontinus lived 140 years after the events, and in his work, *Strategematicon*, he was aiming to give examples of military strategy. He was also Governor of Britain c.74 AD. The story about Commius escaping by employing the strategy of

---

1. Strategemata Bk 2, De Effugiendo. 11 *Commius Atrabas, cum victus a Divo Iulio ex Gallia in Brittanniam fugeret et forte ad Oceanum vento quidem secundo, sed aestu recedente venisset, quamvis naves in siccis litoribus haererent, pandi nihilominus vela iussit. Quae cum persequens eum Caesar ex longinquo tumentia et flatu plena vidisset, ratus prospero sibi eripi cursu recessit.*

deception, when he supposedly raised the sails while stranded on sand banks, comes from this work.

It is possible that, despite fighting against the Romans at Alesia, Commius was installed as a pro-Roman 'king' in the south of Britain. It was not unusual for former enemies of some influence to be granted a pardon or amnesty, and then given position of power as clients of Rome. King Herod, who features in the New Testament, provides another such example, following the Roman Civil War.

Creighton, for instance, argues that no single narrative is universally accepted and adds that *all the pseudo-historical reconstruction above is our own myth making.*[1] Be this as it may, there can be little doubt that pre-Roman Britain had close ties with Roman Gaul and the area around Calleva was pivotal to future events.

The next question concerns the ethnicity of the tribes occupying the lands around Reading and the stronghold of Calleva. This is not a problem that needs concern us overmuch. Unless one accepts the minority view that the Belgic tribes, such as the Atrebates, were of non-Celtic, Germanic, origins, it is clear that all the occupants of the area, no matter which tribe, were Celts.

---

1. Creighton, J. *Coins and power in Late Iron Age Britain*, Cambridge University Press, 2000.

CHAPTER 3

ROMAN BRITAIN

Rome and Britain 51 BC – 43 AD

The ancient history of the fort that became Calleva is unknown. The Celtic word Calleva may have meant a *wooded place.* Underneath Calleva Atrebatum, (Calleva of the Atrebates), there are the remains of a town, built on a grid system, which predates the arrival of the Romans. The existence of a pre-Roman town was proposed by Aileen Fox in 1948.[1] She based her hypothesis on the observation that some of the buildings *were placed obliquely to the known grid* and so belonged to an earlier phase of the town's development than that of the Roman period.

In the late 1960s and 70s this was followed up by Boon, who agreed that it was a more than likely hypothesis.[2] There was also evidence of imported wine and olive oil: signs of a Mediterranean culture associated with Roman influence. It has therefore been suggested that this was consequent on the arrival of the Romanised Atrebates under Commius, possibly duplicating their previous town and capital, Nemetocenna.

In 2011, archaeologists from the University of Reading uncovered what appeared to be the first Iron Age planned town in Britain and so confirmed the above hypothesis. The following is a description of the town as it may have developed and appeared in the 1st century AD.

> *The Inner Earthwork, constructed c.1 AD, enclosed an area of 32ha, and a more extensive series of earthworks were present in the wider area. Small areas of Late Iron Age occupation were uncovered on the south side of the Inner Earthwork and around the South Gate. More detailed evidence for Late Iron Age occupation was excavated below the Forum-Basilica. Several roundhouses, wells and pits were present on a north-east/south -west alignment, dated to c.25BC-15BC. Subsequent occupation, dated to c. 15 BC - AD 40/50, consisted of metalled streets, rubbish pits and palisaded enclosures. Imported Gallo-Belgic fine-wares, amphorae and iron and copper-alloy brooches show that the settlement was high status. Also*

---

1. Quoted by John Wacher, in *The Towns of Roman Britain p256-257*
2. Boon, George *Silchester, the Roman Town of Calleva*

> *distinctive evidence for food was identified, including oyster shell,*
> *and sherds from amphorae which would have contained olive oil,*
> *fish sauce and wine. Excavation of the Late Iron Age phases have*
> *provided evidence for a substantial boundary ditch c. 40 - 20 BC,*
> *a large rectangular hall c. 25 BC - AD 10 and the laying out of*
> *lanes and new property divisions c. AD 10 - 40/50.[1]*

Following Cassivellaunus' defeat in 54 BC, and Commius' arrival in Britain in 51 BC, it would appear that the power of the Catuvellauni had been curtailed and restricted to an area north of the Thames, with Calleva as the centre of Atrebatic power, immediately south of the Thames. The area of influence of the Atrebates tribe possibly included the Belgae and Regnenses tribes, or sub-tribes.[2] The Thames appears to have formed the northern boundary between the lands of the Atrebates and Catuvellauni. If this were so, then the confluence of the Kennet and Thames, and so any settlement at what is today's Reading, would have been at an important border point.[3]

KINGS OF THE ATREBATES AND CATUVELLAUNI	
Kings of the Atrebates	**Kings of the Catuvellauni**
Commius the Gaul 51-30? BC	**Cassivellaunus,** a military leader and possibly chieftain, often associated with the Catuvellauni c. 54 BC
(**Commius son of Commius?** 35 -20 BC)	
Tincomaros (Tincommius, Son of Commius) 25 -20 BC	**Tasciovanus,** c. 20 BC-9 AD
Eppillus 10 BC-10 AD (Son of Commius, brother of Tincommius)	
Verica 10-43 AD (Son of Commius, brother of Tincommius)	
Epaticcus 35 AD (Brother of Cunobelinus, a Catuvellaunian, not therefore from the Atrebates tribe)	**Cunobelinus,** 9-40 AD (Brother of Epaticcus)
Caratacus (Caradog—Caradoc –Caractatus) 43-51 AD (Son of Cunobelinus, a Catuvellaunian, not therefore from the Atrebates tribe)	**Togodumnus** d. 43 AD (Son of Cunobelinus)
	Caratacus 43-51 AD (Son of Cunobelinus)
Cogidubnus 43 AD- 80 ? AD (Client king under the Romans)	

---

1. Fulford, Michael. *City of the Dead: Calleva Atrebatum.*
2. The actual name of this tribe or sub-tribe is the subject of dispute, but as we shall see it is likely that the southern *oppidum* of Noviomagus (Chichester) became the capital of the Atrebates after the Roman Conquest. See following pages in this Chapter.
3. For a detailed look at these tribal lands see Salway, *Tom Hassall Lecture. 1997, 'Roman Oxfordshire'.*

The Relationship between Rome and the Atrebates

Examining something of this history helps us better to understand the peoples that lived in and around the area we now call Reading, just before and during the early stages of the Roman occupation of southern Britain. In a later chapter we shall see to what extent this changed in the century or so prior to the Roman withdrawal in the early years of the 5th century AD.

There is some question as to whether Commius ruled to 20 BC or whether he had a son, also called Commius, who succeeded him. It is feasible that Commius the Gaul lived to 25-20 BC. His sons (see chart opposite) may then have inherited the position in order of seniority. It is also possible that Tincomaros had governed the more southerly area of the Atrebatic lands, with his capital at Noviomagus, (Chichester).

This latter area is usually identified as being the land of the Regnenses tribe, possibly a sub-tribe of the Atrebates. If this is the case, then Tincomaros' brother, Eppillus, may have ruled the northern area jointly with their father. It is possible that in c.20 BC, with the death of his father, Tincomaros became ruler of the whole area. It would also appear that Tincomaros was much more favourably disposed to the Romans, and that he made a treaty with them in 5 AD. Moreover, the numismatic evidence indicates increasingly closer ties with Rome. The types of coins come more to resemble those of Rome, with similar alloy content. It has also been argued that the imagery on the coins may indicate that Tincomaros had been brought up in Rome as an *obsess,* that is, a diplomatic hostage.[1]

Around 7 or 8 AD, this increasing alliance with Rome may have been the reason why Tincomaros was replaced by his brother Eppillus. Tincomaros fled to Rome, apparently seeking Augustus Caesar's support to re-instate him. Whether Augustus ever intended to help Tincomaros, or not, the fact is that he recognised Eppillus as *rex,* king. However, there was evident discord among the Atrebates as a faction opposed to Eppillus' seizure of power supported his younger brother, Verica. The latter led a revolt against Eppillus, who fled through the Regnenses territory and, with his forces, took control of the Cantiaci lands.

---

1. Creighton, John. *Coins and Power in Late Iron Age Britain.* These ancient coins are often referred to as *staters.* This is derived from the Greek word στατήρ (stater) meaning a weight. Originally staters were silver stamped coins dating from the 8th century BC and circulating in various Greek regions up to about 50 AD. Athens, in the late 4th and early 5th centuries, issued bronze coins. Aristophanes refers to these in *The Frogs* and *Ecclesiazusae.* There is some debate as to whether these were silver or even gold plated. One theory is that the Celts, who had spread their influence as far afield as Galatia (Turkey) and Greece, brought the concept of coined money to central Europe and to Gaul. Another possibility is that they had contact with Greek colonies in the western Mediterranean and possibly in southern France. By the 5th c. BC it is likely that the Celts also struck staters from gold but also bronze. The term was then applied to coinage in general.

Possibly sensing an opportunity to re-establish their dominance, the Catuvellauni, under Cunobellinus, began to press the Atrebatic territories. Around 25 AD Verica was forced to retreat and Epaticcus, brother of Cunobellinus, occupied Calleva. Verica continued the struggle so that about 35 AD, when Epaticcus died, Verica made some headway in reconquering his lost lands.

This was a short-lived success as Verica was finally defeated by Caratacus in 41 AD, and fled to Rome. Verica 'appealed to Caesar' for help, and this gave the Emperor, Claudius, the excuse he needed to invade Britain.[1] The main force landed somewhere along the south coast, possibly in a 'friendly' area controlled by the Atrebates. Some of this tribe saw the Romans as a counterbalance to the Catuvellauni.

There is an alternative view that the Romans first landed at Richborough in Kent. The Roman forces, under Aulius Plautius, and later Ostorius Scapula, steadily took possession of Britain. Following Caratacus' defeat and capture, a client kingdom under Cogidubnus, possibly Verica's son, was established, certainly in the territory of the Regnenses, and maybe in the whole of the Atrebatic lands.[2] Some scholars suggest a multi-front invasion.

A far more radical proposition states that Britain's southern rulers were 'Romanised' before the Claudian invasion, welcomed the 'conquest', and profited from it afterwards. In this hypothesis, not only was Cogidubnus 'master of an expanded realm', but he was engaged with the Romans in 'fostering the growth of self-governing towns'. This view is in contradiction to Tacitus' account of an enslaved people; rather it was a joint enterprise by a people who looked to enjoy the privileges of Roman citizenship.[3]

---

1. Cassius Dio *Roman History* Bk LX 19.1   *While these events were happening in the city, Aulus Plautius, a senator of great renown, made a campaign against Britain; for a certain Bericus (Verica?), who had been driven out of the island as a result of an uprising, had persuaded Claudius to send a force thither.* Because the name Verica appears differently in Cassius Dio it is worth seeing the original Greek version: ἐν μὲν δὴ τῇ πόλει ταῦτ᾽ ἐγίγνετο, κατὰ δὲ τὸν αὐτὸν τοῦτον χρόνον Αὖλος Πλαύτιος βουλευτὴς λογιμώτατος ἐς τὴν Βρεττανίαν ἐστράτευσε: **Βέρικος** γάρ τις ἐκπεσὼν ἐκ τῆς νήσου κατὰ στάσιν ἔπεισε τὸν Κλαύδιον δύναμιν ἐς αὐτήν. For Cassius Dio's full account of the conquest see *Roman History* Bk LX 19-23. There is no V in Greek hence **B** represents the nearest sound.

2. Tacitus *Agricola* 1.14 *Some of the states were given to king Cogidumnus,* (see * below) *who lived down to our day a most faithful ally.* Quaedam civitates Cogidumno regi donatae (is ad nostram usque memoriam fidissimus mansit). For a full description of Caratacus' defeat and his subsequent treatment by the Romans see Tacitus Annals Book XII. (*There is some dispute as to whether Cogidumnus is the same as Togodumnus or Cogidubnus, or whether these are all different transliterations of the same person). For discussion about who Cogibubnus may have been see Wacher *The Towns of Roman Britain* especially Ch 6. The lands of the Regnenses were centred on today's Chichester, Sussex and Hampshire.

3. British Archaeology 37 Sept 1998. Martin Henig *Togidubnus and the Roman liberation*. Togidubnus is an alternative spelling of Cogidubnus.

A Citizen of Rome

This brings us to the issue of what it meant to be Roman citizen or a person living under the rule of Rome. Just as today the layman should enter into the legal arena with great care, the same applies when looking at such a complex system of jurisprudence as was developed by Rome over several centuries. The problem is further complicated by the fact that over this period the laws regarding 'citizenship' were not static. During both the Republic and the Empire, contemporary Roman jurists debated the question of what constituted the right to 'citizenship', its different levels, the relationship between Rome and the peoples of the territories that it occupied, and the rights and duties each had one to another.[1]

Gaius (c.130-180 AD), one such commentator, divided society as follows.[2] All people within the Roman territories were either slaves or free. If the latter, then they were either born free (*ingenui*) or were freedmen (*libertini*). In simplified terms their civic status could be that of a Roman citizen, a *coloniarius* or a member of a third category, which did not confer full citizenship, but neither were they slaves. These were known as *peregrini.*

The first two groups, *ingenui* and *libertini,* were subject to the rights and duties of a full Roman citizen. Their final court of appeal in law was the Emperor or his delegate. They could not be tortured or whipped; they could own and inherit property; they were exempt from certain taxes; they could hold offices of state and enter the military.

The third group, the *peregrini,* was by far the largest in the early years of the Empire (1st Century AD). Although this entailed recognition that they were not slaves, the *peregrini* did not share the civic rights afforded to Roman citizens, such as protection against torture or flogging. They were also liable for an annual poll tax (*tributum capitis*). Roman citizens were exempt from this. *Peregrini* could not own land, nor enter the army, except as auxiliaries.

Full citizenship had been gradually extended under the Republic. First it was expanded territorially. Following the *Social War,* (90-88 BC), most of Italy, south of the River Po, came under Roman jurisdiction. With the inclusion of many more tribes and their lands under Julius Caesar, (c.49 BC), and the creation of more colonies and *Municipia* beyond the Italian peninsula, citizenship was granted to some, but by no means all, of the native inhabitants. In these cases citizenship was frequently conferred on the aristocratic elite and soldiers.

---

1. Vainyte, Gird. *Roman Law, Roman Citizenship, Roman Identity?* (MA Thesis Leiden University 2014).
2. Gaius *Institutiones 1. 9-12*

Very often the governance of the new 'colony' was handed over to the local chief or the previous aristocracy, especially if they had co-operated with Rome. Likewise the magistrates, who were responsible for the implementation of Roman law, were granted citizenship, as were the local senators or councillors.[1]

In this way Rome assured itself of the support of the legal and military elite. Consequently the majority of the 'conquered' population found themselves distanced legally, socially and economically from their erstwhile compatriots, and now rulers.

With the passage of time, acquisition of citizenship became easier until, in 212 AD, the Emperor Caracalla granted full citizenship to all free subjects of the Empire. This action improved the legal status of the ordinary person throughout the Roman world.

However, economically this brought with it new responsibilities. Although full citizenship initially removed the burden of the poll tax, (Roman citizens were exempt from this), it did entail its replacement with other taxes such as the *tributum soli* or land tax. When Diocletian (282-305 AD) reformed the tax system, it would appear that a poll tax was once again in force.[2]

---

1. Frere, Sheppard. *Britannia p182-183*
2. Dio Cassius. Bk LXXV111. 9. See also Duncan-Jones, Richard (1994) *Money & Government in the Roman Empire*

Numismatic record of the tribal leaders of the Atrebates and Catuvellauni.

Commius the Gaul 51-30? BC
Found at Reading

(Commius son of Commius? 35-20 BC)   No definitive record

Tincomaros (Tincommius)

Tasciovanus

Eppillus 10 BC-10 AD

Verica 10-43 AD

Cunobellinus

Epaticcus 35-43 AD

Caratacus (Caradog)
43-51 AD

Cogidubnus 43 AD

Temple plaque to Minerva and Neptune erected by
authority of Cogidubnus (below left). Inserted missing
letters in brackets in the Latin transcription.

This translates as:

*To Neptune and Minerva, for the
welfare of the Divine House, by the
authority of Tiberius Claudius
Cogidubnus, great king of the Britons,
the guild of smiths and those in it
gave this temple at their own
expense ... ens, son of Pudentinus,
presented the forecourt.*

NEPTVNO·ET MINERVAE
TEMPLVM
PRO·SALVTE·DOMVSDIVINAE
EX·AVCTORITATE·TIB·CLAVD·
COGIDVBNIREG·MAGNBRIT·
COLEGIVMFABRORETQVI·IN·EO
SVNT·D·S·D·DONANTEAREAM
ENTE·PVDENTINI·FIL

(N)EPTVNO ET MINERVAE
TEMPLVM
(PRO) SALVTE DO(MUS) DIVIN(AE)
(EX) AVCTORITAT(E) (TIB) CLAVD
(CO) GIDVBNI R(EG) (MA) GN BRIT
(COLE)GIUM FABRORE(T) (Q)VI IN E(O)
(SVNT) D S D DONANTE AREAM
ENTE PVDENTINI FIL

The Atrebatic Client Kingdom

If even a part of what many commentators, both contemporary and later, write, is accurate, then Cogidubnus and the Atrebates were a significant factor in the arrival of the Romans. It would appear that although Cogidubnus' capital was at *Noviomagus Reginorum* (Chichester),[1] the town of *Calleva* (Silchester) also grew in importance. We have seen that Calleva already existed as an Iron Age town controlled by the Atrebates clan or tribe, certainly following the arrival of Commius around 50 BC.

There can be little doubt that an earlier Celtic, or Belgic, tribe was already in possession of the area south of the Thames; maybe these peoples were related to the Belgic Atrebeans.[2] It is also possible, however, that their roots lay in one of the earlier waves of Celtic settlers. It is, of course, also possible that the groups intermingled. Before the arrival of the Romans it would appear that the Thames created a frontier between the expanding Catuvellauni and the peoples south of the river. Calleva was in all probability the main semi-fortified settlement of the area. As we have seen, excavations at Silchester reveal a pre-Roman 'town', much smaller than the later Calleva Atrebatum.[3]

By the turn of the first century AD, Calleva had an inner earthwork enclosing about 32ha. There was a more extensive series of earthworks in the wider surrounding area. There is ample evidence of late Iron Age occupation on the south side of the Inner Earthwork and around the South Gate.[4]

Below the Forum-Basilica, more archaeological evidence has been found of a late Iron Age settlement. Moreover, several roundhouses, wells and pits were discovered on a north-east / south-west alignment. These have been dated to between c.25 BC and c.15 BC. As the first century progressed, up to and including the Roman invasion, there is more solid evidence of Gallo-Belgic occupation. The existence of metalled streets, rubbish pits and palisaded enclosures, imported Gallo-Belgic fineware, amphorae and iron and copper-alloy brooches all indicate a high status settlement.

---

1. Noviomagus Reginorum: This is a hybrid word comprising both Latin and Celtic elements. It is usually translated as *new fields* from the Latin *novus = new* and the Celtic *magus = field*. Alternatively *Magus* in Latin means *wise, learned, clever* as in the *Three Magi*. There are several other places called Noviomagus and so the title *Reginorum,* or versions of this, was added to distinguish it from other similarly named towns. It has been proposed that the famous excavations at Fishbourne may be of Cogidubnus' palace.
2. We have already examined the debate concerning the ethnicity of these peoples, pages 17-19.
3. Fulford, M. and Timby, J. 2000. *Late Iron Age and Roman Silchester: Excavations on the Site of the Forum Basilica*, 1977, 1980-86. London: Society for the Promotion of Roman Studies. Britannia Monograph Series No. 15
4. Boon, G. *Roman Silchester* and Fulford, M. 1984. *Silchester: Excavations on the Defences 1974-80*. London: Society for Antiquaries. Britannia Monograph Series No. 5

It is worth comparing the numismatic record with the archaeology. Examples of Commius' coins, with their distinctive feature: the horse with its tail split into three on the reverse, are not to be found along the southern coast.[1] If this is where Commius landed, then it is something of an anomaly, especially as they do appear in the Middle Thames Valley, centred on Reading. This would indicate a significant presence around Reading of Commius and his followers.

The question is whether this area was dominated by the Atrebates or the Catuvellauni. We know that the latter continued to press the Atrebates further south until finally Verica was forced to flee to Rome. It has been argued that the defence works at Calleva were either an initial attempt to halt the Catuvellauni by the Atrebates or, alternatively, the Catuvellauni, having captured Calleva, reinforced it against a possible counter-attack by Verica or even against the invading Romans in 43 AD.

The presence of Catuvellauni coins, both of Cunobellinus and of Epatticus, reflects the advances made by the Catuvellauni against the Atrebates in the Thames Valley. Whatever the reason for the construction of these pre-Roman earthworks, the numismatic evidence indicates that the borderlands of the Thames, and so the area we known as Reading, were of major importance.

We have seen that the people living here may have been of mixed background: Atrebatic and pre-Atrebatic. It would not be unreasonable to speculate that, as the Catuvellauni took control of the area, they also settled the land. In all cases the advancing Roman force, supporting the Atrebatic Cogidubnus, would have encountered the indigenous, most probably Celtic, people.

By endorsing Cogidubnus as a client king, Rome was making a clear statement as to where its preferences lay. Caratacus, a Catuvellauni, had fought and lost against Rome. There is some debate as to how long Cogidubnus reigned. He proved a constant and faithful ally to Rome. He did not support the Boudiccan uprising, and he is singled out for this by Tacitus.[2] Whilst it is likely that his capital remained at Noviomagus (Chichester), Calleva grew in importance.

Although Calleva's main era of expansion was not until later, there is evidence that a forum, the amphitheatre and baths were constructed in the 1st century AD. As Boon says, around thirty-three buildings, including the bath house, appear to be in line, joining the east-west entrances of the inner earthwork.[3]

1. Boon, G. *ibid p 45-47*. Of course it may be that such specimens have yet to be discovered.
2. See page 26 note 2
3. Aileen Fox in 1948 (*Anitiquity xxii p172)* first proposed this Iron Age town with a grid–like street system. Its relationship with the earthworks was at the time unknown as these were only uncovered at few years later. Among other remains of the pre-Roman town, which follow the older street lay out, are several Romano-Celtic temples. (Wacher, J. *The Towns of Roman Britain p268*).

These buildings pre-date the later Roman grid-based buildings. If the existence of a tile from the bath house with Emperor Nero's (53-68 AD) name indicates not just approval but a connection with the very pinnacle of Roman power, then not only were these baths among the first to be built in Britain, but they demonstrate the close alliance between the Atrebates and Rome.[1]

Frere has pointed out that in Gaul, although *peregrini* towns and those associated with former 'client kingdoms', were not necessarily looked upon as *municipia,* they often did become the *origo* of future citizens of the Empire and took on the role of *civitates.* He further argues that, especially following the extension of citizenship in 210 AD, this process was also likely to have occurred in Britain.[2]

At Calleva, the existence of a twice than life-size bronze statue in one of the temples might indicate the complete Romanisation of the area, not just its status as a 'conquered' territory. If we add to this mix the indications of a prosperous *peregrinus* class, as indicated by the existence of a Guild of Peregrini, *(Collegium peregrinorum*), we can see, in the developing town, a centre of considerable importance, fully Romanised, yet under the administration of its local Celtic peoples.[3] There appears to be little evidence that Calleva ever achieved the status of *municipium* but it was a *civitas peregrina.* Estimates of its population range widely, from as low as 600 to as high as 7500 people, and it served as the *civitas* or administrative centre for the area, as the main market town and the centre for the surrounding estates. It has been suggested that the lack of villas around Calleva indicates that the land was in fact farmed from this centre.[4]

Whether this was the case in the 1st century AD, or whether, as the centuries progressed, the extent of farming reached well beyond the immediate neighbourhood of Calleva, there can be little doubt about the importance of the town culturally, socially and economically. The surrounding countryside would have benefitted from the increased trade and goodwill this status brought.

---

1. In 2016 further excavations cast doubt on the existence of a large building in this north-east area. Rather, what were believed to be foundation trenches robbed of their walls, turned out to be unfinished foundations. The area seems to have been avoided at the time for the next two centuries. Professor Fulford speculated that the 'Nero tile' may have come from the municipal bath complex: an early feature in the Roman town plan. In 2019 excavations continued to determine the timescale of the baths. See *Current Archaeology* Jan. 2020.

2. Frere, Sheppard. *Britannia Ch 9*

3. Fragments from around the temple in *insula xxxv* refer to this *collegium.* There have been two explanations for this. One is that it refers to a sufficient number of non-Callevans in the town to form a guild and erect a monument in the temple. The other explanation is that the word *perigrinorum* refers to the legal status of this group of inhabitants. (Wacher p274). Whichever is true, the existence of this memorial in a temple just at the north gate of the town does show the growing influence of the town in the area and its relationship with the surrounding inhabitants.

4. Boon, G. *Roman Silchester p178* and Fulford, M. *Calleva Atrebatum,* 1987.

CHICHESTER: NOVIOMAGUS, FISHBOURNE AND BIGNOR

Near to Chichester the opulent Roman villas at Fishbourne and Bignor were clearly the homes of very powerful people. It is generally agreed that the earliest residences date to the 1st century AD, but their additions and lavish mosaics are of a much later period, some maybe even to the late 3rd century.

Whether either could have been connected with the Atrebatic stronghold of Noviomagus remains a disputed point. Barry Cunliffe, when first excavating Fishbourne, suggested that the early building may have been Cogidubnus' palace. Other, revisionist, theories have since been proposed. For instance, Miles Russell believes that Fishbourne, as a whole, may date from a much later period.

Some theories suggest that the client Atrebatic kingdom under Cogidubnus was divided on his death. Wacher proposes that eight new *civitates* were created in the last twenty years of the 1st century AD, and that each of these would have required administrative capitals. In the case of Cogidubnus' kingdom, Wacher says that three such sites were chosen: Noviomagus (Chichester), Venta Belgarum (Winchester) and Calleva Atrebatum (Silchester).[1]

If this is true, then the northern area of the old Atrebatic tribe, with its centre at Calleva, would have increased in importance, as would have the hinterland it controlled, including the confluence of the rivers Thames and Kennet. Indeed, owing to the complexity of the Roman administrative machine, as the Diocese of Britannia became established over the next two centuries, the same would have held hold true even if Calleva did not become such a capital.[2]

In the next section we shall see just how Calleva was linked with its own immediate hinterland and to the rest of Rome's newly acquired territory.

---

1. Wacher, John. *The Towns of Roman Britain Ch 1*. See page 56 for an explanation of the political structure of the Roman Empire.
2. For an explanation of the administrative divisions of Britain see page 57 and Appendix F page 124.

Roman Settlements in and around Reading

There is ample evidence for a significant Roman presence around Reading. Romano-British artefacts are plentiful and well documented.[1] As Slade comments, concentrations of sherds have been discovered at Tilehurst, Southcote, Reading Market Place and in the area just to the east of the Thames-Kennet confluence. The central part of the town itself has been less productive. This may be due to subsequent building and disturbance, as much as to the absence of a Roman presence. A Romano-British cemetery was also discovered just to the east of Reading.[2] It was normal Roman practice to bury the dead outside the city walls. Whether the existence of such a cemetery warrants the conclusion that it was attached to a town is open to dispute. Nevertheless it does indicate at least a degree of intensity of local settlements.

Indeed, from the 18th century, so much Roman material was found around the confluence of the Thames and Kennet that, before Silchester was identified as *Calleva Atrebatum*, many antiquarians believed Reading had been this major *oppidum*.[3] They even identified the name Coley as being derived from Calleva.

Looking further afield, studies of the Roman road system, and its associated known habitations, present conflicting evidence about Reading's socio-economic role. On the one hand, even a cursory glance at the map of southern Britain shows the pivotal position of Calleva Atrebatum. Yet there are anomalies which require examination.

The map opposite shows the Roman road pattern in southern Britain and its linking communication hubs. Calleva is arguably at its centre. Not surprisingly the map demonstrates how major settlements tend to congregate along the roads. If we examine the course of the Thames we can see that, although no road is marked, there must have been roads to reach the concentration of settlements which appears on the east-west axis between Pontes, (Staines), and Reading. Yet these settlements run in a line further north than the known Roman Road (Iter V11) leading from Pontes to Calleva Atrebatum.

1. See Reading Museum's catalogue.

2. Stevens J. *Discovery of an Ancient Cemetery in Reading*. BAJ 1895 Journal 1. The burials here appear to span several hundreds of years, from pre-Roman to Saxon times, as we shall see in greater detail later. In ERW p95 there is a report of human remains in the Crane Wharf area, with radio carbon dating of between 1-340 AD

3. Reynolds, in his commentary of the *Iter Britannarium* identifies Calleva with Reading. *Iter VII* pp286-296. This is an interesting study as it also catalogues, and analyses, the versions and commentaries of the *Iter*, looking at its history from the time of Leland, Camden, Stukeley and Horsley among others. He notes that Leland considered Reading to be the *Pontes* of Roman times and that Horsley believed Silchester to be the site of Calleva.

The archaeology of the Romano-British period indicates that there were groups of people in the Reading area, but living in scattered settlements. The rivers, especially the Thames, possibly provided for a degree of local trade, but: *the proximity of the important cantonal capital of Calleva Atrebatum and the avoidance of the area by major roads were economic factors that could not be overcome. The area can at the most have been a 'pagus', a rural unit of local government, within the 'civitas' of the Atrebates.*[1]

On Map A, over the page, the superimposed dark line joins the known Roman settlements, villas and large houses, which lay within the large bend in the Thames between Reading and Windsor, sometimes referred to as the 'Henley Loop'. As Slade says: *although, therefore, there is no record of a Roman road passing through Reading the existence of Roman and pre-Roman settlements in the area suggest some form of road infrastructure.*[2]

In the 1960s and 70s a study of the Henley Loop showed that *the distribution between one villa and another is almost invariably one and half miles, with one or two exceptions.*[3] Likewise, along the river banks it was estimated that villas had about a mile, to a mile and a half, frontage, resulting in 450 to 600 working acreage for each farm.

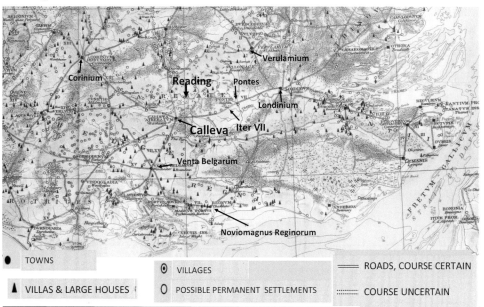

● TOWNS	◉ VILLAGES	═══ ROADS, COURSE CERTAIN
▲ VILLAS & LARGE HOUSES	O POSSIBLE PERMANENT SETTLEMENTS	┈┈ COURSE UNCERTAIN

1. Slade C. *Historic Towns—Reading*. It is worth noting that Slade considers Calleva to have had the status of a civitas.
2. Ibid. The term *villa* has been used by various writers in this context to include some of the larger Roman houses and farms in the area.
3. Over L. *Roman Villa Settlement in the Middle Thames Valley* 1970

MAP A

It has been argued that the consistency of this pattern indicates some degree of control by the Roman authorities, who would also have demanded a percentage of the produce, especially for the support of its troops. It is unlikely that such a pattern would have been part of the previous Celtic agricultural system.

A logical corollary to such a degree of intensive farming, and its associated produce, would have been the need for transportation. This could have been by either river or road. If the former, then, downriver, produce would most certainly have been taken to *Pontes*, (Staines), which, as a major town, was on the main arterial road between Londinium and Calleva, (*Iter VII*). it is also possible that, upriver, produce could have been brought to Reading. We shall see shortly that there is some evidence of wharves on the northern banks of the Thames at Caversham and possibly on the Kennet in the east of Reading.

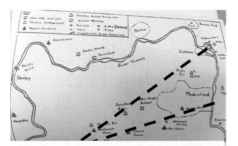

MAP B. *The Henley Loop with major known Roman archaeological remains. The dotted lines are suggested possible routes of the 'lost' Camlet Way.*

What is certain is that there would have been a road system capable of transporting this precious agricultural produce. As most of the villas and farms were within the loop, and not on the river bank, it was essential to have a workable road network. A significant degree of speculation exists about its nature. There may have been a number of small 'commercial roads' leading to major routes as outlined on Map A. It has been suggested that the lost 'Camlet Way' passed through this area.[1] If this is so, we are looking at one of Rome's major arterial/military roads, which would have linked Camulodunum (Colchester), Verulamium (St Albans) and Calleva (Silchester). Its existence would not detract from the theory that there were

---

1. This is the same route as suggested by Seaby BAJ 36, 1932. *Knowl Hill excavations.* See also www.marlowarchaeology.org/Pages/CamletWay.aspx and *Bucks, Berks and Oxon Archaeological Journal: p76. 1926.* The conclusion by Andy Ford says that *It is possible that the river itself acted as a major form of communication and transport, and that is reinforced by evidence from other villas along the Thames. But it is equally unlikely that the villas would have operated successfully without some form of network of land-based communications and transport, no matter how rudimentary these roads might have been.*

lesser commercial roads linked with it. On the contrary, following Agricola's orders, forums were built in towns as social and economic foci of the areas they administered. These forums were to be places of trade, as well as of administration, and demonstrated the economic, as well as the political, power of Rome.[1]

Whether or not the Camlet Way existed, what is certain is that the Thames Valley within the Henley Loop was a heavily farmed and populated area. Moreover its two pivotal points were Pontes to the east, where the river swings northwards, and today's Reading on the westerly base of the great arc of the Thames. The question is to what extent 'Reading' was a trading port.

When discussing the Roman road system we are confronted with the problem that it is commonly assumed that there is a great deal of reliable information about this topic.[2] This is not altogether true. Initially our knowledge depends on the Antonine Itinerary, (*Itinerarium Antonini Augusti*, 'The Roads of the Emperor Antoninus'). However, there is considerable dispute about the reliability of this source, not least because of Bertram's 18th century forgery *De Situ Britanniae*.[3]

Today, research and revisionist theories are challenging many of the preconceptions, not just about the Roman invasion but about the nature of the occupation of Britain, and the relationship between the local native tribes and the Romans. This, of course, includes a reappraisal of the economy of the country, its supporting infrastructure and whether pre-invasion Britain already had a more developed economy than previously postulated, including a workable road system. All this is a far cry from the picture of a savage, uncivilised, druidic culture.

Turning again to the Reading area, there can be little doubt about just how widespread Roman settlements, or maybe we should say, Roman-controlled settlements, were in the Thames Valley. Consequently it is not surprising that north of the river, in Caversham, significant finds have been made in several places.

These include the 1965 discoveries near Old Grove House in Emmer Green. The archaeology here ranges from pre-Roman Iron Age metal objects and pottery, to 4th century bronze coins. The Emmer Green excavation produced sherds spanning several hundred years, from pre-Roman to late Romano-British times.

1. Over L. *Roman Villa Settlement*
2. Margary I. *The Roman Roads in Britain*
3. In 1747 Charles Bertram claimed to have discovered a map of Roman Britain copied from original sources by a 14th century medieval monk, Richard of Gloucester. This showed eighteen previously unknown Roman roads or itineraries. The hoax was only exposed nearly 100 years later.

In addition to the bronze coins, it uncovered hob nails, sandal cleats, nails, a bronze bracelet and a knife blade. This has led to the interpretation that the site was in continuous occupation from pre-Roman times.

The lack of high status archaeology, such as Samian ware and Roman tiling, has led some commentators to believe that this was predominantly a low status, possibly 'native', British site.[1] In other words there exists sufficient archaeological evidence to postulate continuous settlement in this part of Emmer Green from pre-Roman times and throughout the Roman period; but evidence is lacking for any detailed conclusions.[2]

That Caversham was widely settled is witnessed by other finds, such as the pottery excavated in 1924 in All Hallows Road. This lies on the way out of Caversham towards Henley. Deans Farm, on the north bank of the Thames near its confluence with the Kennet, has provided another insight, into what may well have been an early Christian household. Here, in 1988, a circular lead tank was discovered in a well. It had been crushed and was decorated with the Chi-Rho symbol.[3] This is commonly associated with Christianity, and so probably dates from the mid to late 4th century AD, when the resurgence of anti-Christian pagan cults forced many Christians to hide the symbols of their faith.[4]

There is also evidence that some sort of wharf, or landing stage, existed in the cutting at this point in the river Thames. Its exact size and importance are unknown, but it could well have served the hinterland of the area that today we know as Caversham. Another hypothesis, and one alluded to above, is that this served as a wharf for agricultural produce from bank-side Henley Loop farms. It would also be logical to infer that, if produce was being transported by water, then there may have been a larger wharf to the south of the Thames. This, as in medieval times, may have been on the Kennet rather than on the Thames. The topographical nature of the land, with the southern banks of the Thames liable to flooding, make this a plausible hypothesis.

1. *Samian Ware* or *terra sigillata* is high quality Roman pottery identifiable by its red, brown or yellowish colouring and distinctive satin slip-ware texture. Its name probably derives from the colour of clay of the island of Samos. Its main centre of production was Aretium; it is sometimes called Aretium ware, (Arezzo, Italy), and was exported throughout the Roman Empire, especially around the Mediterranean. By the late 1st century it was bring produced in Gaul at Les Martres-de Veyre and Lezoux and subsequently in some British towns. The quality of the latter is inferior to that produced in Italy.

2. *Emmer Green Past and Present* (Emmer Green Residents Association, 2001)

3. This is made up of the two Greek letters: X (pronounced kai and usually transliterated as CH in English) and P (this is the letter R and pronounced *row* as in the word *crow*). They are the first two letters of the name of Christ in Greek—Χριστός

4. Guy, C. *Roman Circular Lead Tanks in Britain.* Britannia XII 1981. (It is in the possession of Reading Museum.)

The Kennet lends itself more readily to year-round transportation. Moreover, Thames traffic would have had easy access to the Kennet. These speculative theories merely illustrate some of the possible interpretative variations offered by the infrastructure of the area, which was dominated by Calleva. As in the case of any complex economy, spread as it is over many centuries, several solutions, with some being favoured over others at different times, would have developed to meet the challenges associated with changes in circumstances, such as the vicissitudes of the weather, along with social, economic and political factors.

It is likely, therefore, that Reading's topography, its position as a crossing point, its linkage with the farms both to its east and north, and its place on the Kennet, would all contribute to making it an important hub, with links to the Roman settlements of Dorchester to the north-west, and to the rich agricultural land of the Henley Loop to its east.

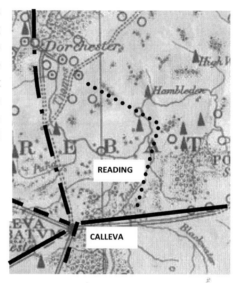

Margary's road network.	
Minor branches	— · —
Main routes	————
Principal branches	— — —
Minor branch road	··········

So can we make an informed estimate about the road layout over the period of Roman occupation? Margary's 1973 version places a minor branch road leading north from the main Londinium-Calleva route near today's Stratfield Saye and skirting Reading to the east, following the Thames along the south bank, crossing near Henley and so moving west towards Dorchester. He does not mention the suggested Camlet Way, which we saw earlier, but either of the routes shown on MAP B (page 36) would fit in with Margary's hypothesis. Moreover, either one of these would also match the *viator* from Verulamium which Margary proposes on his full map of Britian.[1]

The existence of a cemetery[2] containing Roman remains in the area of today's Cemetery Junction, to the east of Reading, adds an extra factor for consideration. At the time of its discovery, in 1890, Stevens concluded that it

---

1. Margary I *Roman Roads in Britain*. 1973. The *viatores*, (plural of *'viator'*), only exist north of London.

2. Stevens, J. *The Discovery of an Ancient Cemetery in Reading*, (p 35).

was a burial ground of *early date and lengthened usage*. Some of the graves gave indications of Christian Romano-British occupation. The absence of military equipment, and the use of lead and pewter for ornaments, implied a settled people but with little wealth. The physical characteristics of some of the skeletons, claimed Stevens, were indicative of Celtic origins. There was also evidence of later Christian Saxon burials. We shall look at this in more detail later.

The existence of a substantial non-military cemetery in this location is, as Stevens says, an indication of a settled farming community, probably labourers, on the nearby estates. What is significant, in attempting to determine the road infrastructure, is its proximity to Margary's proposed route leading from Calleva to the Henley Loop. It is just possible that this was not merely a minor branch road, as Margary claimed, but that it was in fact the continuation of the Camlet Way as described above by Seaby, and as investigated by Marlow Archaeology.

Although a single case study does not prove a general, let alone universal, truth, it is worth looking at one such farm within the Henley Loop. In 1929 at Canhurst Farm, Knowl Hill, between Reading and Maidenhead, a quantity of Romano-British pottery was unearthed. In the subsequent years more artefacts were discovered during excavations. As the archaeology is of low-status material, these were described, at the time, as possibly appertaining to the outbuildings of a larger, but still low-status, house. Only a few pieces of higher quality Samian ware were discovered. Most of the pottery is coarse-ware, made during the 2nd and 3rd centuries; moreover there is an absence of characteristic 4th century types. The conclusion at the time was that the countryside around was *well settled by Romanised Britons.*[1]

Whoever has looked at the pattern of settlements around Reading during the Roman period agrees that some sort of overland transport infrastructure must have existed in the area. The questions are not whether there was a road system, but where it lay and whether it was an integral part of the major arterial network. Further to this is the problem of water travel, if it existed at all, and if so, to what extent, and what role was played by Reading and Caversham in the greater picture of population settlement, local industry and food distribution.

---

1. Seaby W A, *A Romano-British Building at Knowl Hill, Berks.* BAJ 36, 1932.

There is, therefore, sufficient evidence to suggest the existence of a well-settled Romano-British agricultural economy to the east of Reading.

However, much of this is low status and so 'British', rather than Roman.

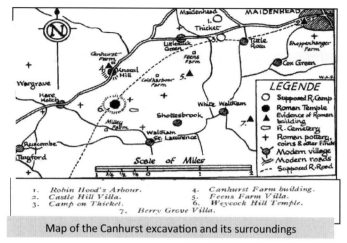

Map of the Canhurst excavation and its surroundings

The settlements would have been served by a comprehensive road system, part of which, most likely, led towards a main arterial road, namely the Camlet Way. It is possible, failing any definite proof, that the Londinium-Calleva road was that principal route. It is not surprising, therefore, that the cemetery lying to the east of Reading, and on the north-south road proposed by Margary, and possibly linked to the vanished Camlet Way, contains evidence of low-status burials for this period in its history.

Even if there was a truly 'Roman Villa', occupied by high status Romans, the inhabitants would have had connections with Calleva and most probably taken their dead there for their funeral rites. It was customary that the body of a very high-status individual should be brought to the forum for a eulogy, a *laudatio*. Roman funerary practices were various and changed over time, and this is not the place to describe them. However, if there were Roman villas, with higher status families, in the Reading area, then it would not be surprising if Calleva, rather than Reading, were the focus of attention.

It is clear that both to the north and east of Reading there is evidence of continual agricultural settlement, with its origins dating to before the Roman occupation and lasting throughout the Roman period. It would seem that this is mainly of low social status and so of continued British, in other words pre-Roman, habitation. It was most certainly part of the hinterland controlled by the *oppidum* of Calleva Atrebatum. As we have seen, there are some indications of early Christianity, as would be expected, following the reforms of Emperor Constantine.[1]

---

1. By the Edict of Milan, 313 AD, Constantine granted freedom of worship in the Western Empire. Licinius, the Eastern Emperor, likewise implemented a similar reform in the Eastern Empire.

Turning to Reading itself, the evidence for Roman occupation is far less abundant. As stated in *Under the Oracle,* up to 1998 there had been only *two previous archaeological projects of any significant scale within the centre of Reading.*[1] Slade's excavations of the Abbey revealed no Roman remains, whilst those by Hawkes and Fasham provided only a few, dating to pre-Saxon times. Nevertheless, they are worth recording. This latter project spanned the best part of a decade and looked at the history of Reading's waterfronts. The importance of this study, both nationally and locally, cannot be overestimated.

Nationally, as Wessex Archaeology pointed out in 1974, Reading offered the *only example in Britain … of an inland (non tidal) waterfront with the potential for detailed examination.* This consisted of 900 metres along the River Kennet, and its associated waterways, leading to the Thames. Along this stretch there was ample historical and archaeological evidence of wharfs, mills and other socio-economic industrial activity, dating back several hundred years. It was also close to the earliest presumed, and known, human habitations around the medieval Abbey and the Minster Church of St Mary, the latter frequently supposed to have been the site of the first, or main, Saxon settlement.

The first phase of Wessex Archaeology's waterfront survey began with excavations in the Abbey Wharf sector, where what are described as *probable Roman tile* deposits were found. These were discovered in a layer below that of early Saxon material, giving an indication of some form of continuous use of the area. It should be noted that, owing to silting and associated human activity, the line of the Kennet tended to move eastwards, so that by the 18th century the river course had shifted significantly further in that direction.

Overall, little evidence of Roman fabric, (that is pottery), or indeed of other artefacts dating to this period, was discovered. As the report states, *the importance... of the earliest evidence in the historic period is easily overstated. Finds of some Roman brick, tile and pottery at Abbey Wharf cannot be ascribed to a known site.*[2] However, the report does note Astill's suggestion that Reading may have served as a river port for Calleva.[3]

---

1. *UO.* Ch 6 p279. These refer to Slade's 1970s excavations of the Abbey and *Excavations on Reading Waterfront Sites, 1979-1988,* Hawkes and Fasham. Wessex Archaeology report no 5, page 14

2. Ibid pp 170 and 191 (For those not familiar with the terminology, the word 'fabric' refers to pottery)

3. Astill, G.G *Historic Towns in Berkshire: An Archaeological Appraisal.* 1978

We saw the suggestion of this possibility above, in connection with the landing stage, or wharf, at Deans Farm, on the northern bank of the Thames. The argument is speculative and based on possibility and likelihood, rather than sound archaeological evidence. The introduction of fish-weirs in the late 12th or early 13th century impaired navigation along the Thames, especially upstream of Henley. The river certainly appears to have been navigable before this period. The 11th century Abingdon Chronicle refers to river traffic between London and Oxford, and the abundance of Taynton quarry stone at Reading Abbey would indicate that the Thames was used for this purpose in the 12th century.[1] It is worth interjecting a note to the effect that we know that, even in Tudor times, the river was in use for transportation of bulky goods. One instance is John London's report to Thomas Cromwell at the time of the Dissolution of the Monasteries in 1538, when he transported by barge the spoils from the shrine of Our Lady of Caversham to London for their destruction.

There are somewhat contrary views about the use of the Thames for major transportation in Roman times. Part of Oxford Archaeology's *Thames though Time* project looked at the role of the river and concluded that it was not a significant resource.[2] However, as we have just seen, others disagree with this assessment. It would almost seem strange if the Romans did not use this economic and appropriate means of transport for bulky goods, at least at a local level. If so, then Reading, as the nearest settlement on the Thames to Calleva, would be the most obvious choice for an inland port, at least for local produce. Whether this was the case or not, it is clear that the areas around Reading, both to its east and north, were settled with farming communities, that it was served by a system of roads, that it possessed at least one major cemetery, and that most of the people were of low status, most likely the descendants of the original pre-Roman inhabitants of the area.

Archaeological evidence of a significant Roman presence in Reading itself is very limited. Where it does exist it is consistent with the possibility that there was a Romano-British settlement to the east of the town. The style of the few fragments of archaeology that were discovered below the Saxon level, accords with other material found in the Thames-Kennet area relating to the Roman period.

---

1. Taynton quarry, on the River Windrush just north west of Oxford, is believed to have been used from Roman times. This quarry's stone was used in many parts of the building of Reading Abbey. It may, of course, have been transported by road.

2. Oxford Archaeology. *The Thames through Time; The Archaeology of the Gravel Terraces of the Upper and Middle Thames,* 2009

We shall see, when looking at the excavations at the east end of the 1121 monastery, that some Romano-British artefacts were found in this area.[1] In 2015 a hoard of about 300 Roman coins was discovered to the south of the town, at the Ridgeway Primary School. These were probably hidden by a fairly prosperous farmer, most likely a Roman. Of some significance is the fact that the site is approximately that of the Bronze Age settlement that we noted above.[2]

In the following chapter we shall look at how and why the Roman domination of Britain came to an end. It was as a consequence, not merely of the collapse of the Roman Empire, but the way in which this occurred, and its impact on different parts of what had been Britannia, that Reading emerged as the main settlement in the Middle Thames Valley.

In other words, to understand the emergence of the settlement that we now call Reading, it is also necessary to examine and understand the fall of Rome.

The events and characters are complicated so to help, below, is a list of the leading figures mentioned in the following chapter.

Alaric - Leader of the Visigoths, responsible for the Sack of Rome 410, d. 410
Arcadius - Son of Theodosius I, Eastern Emperor, d.408
Constantine III - Roman General in the Diocese of Britain. Elected by his army as leader in 407, d. 411
Constantius III - Roman general. Succeeded Honorius as Western Emperor, 421
Flavius Bauto - Romanised Frankish General. Led Emperor Theodosius' forces against Magnus Maximus. His daughter married Emperor Arcadius, d. c385
Gerontius - Roman General. Commander of imperial forces in Hispania d. 411
Gildo - Roman General. Leader of a revolt in Africa in 398
Gratian - Western Emperor and co-Western Emperor with Valentinian, d. 383
Honorius - son of Theodosius I. Responsible for the *Rescript of 410*, d. 423
Magnus Maximus - Elected Commander by his British troops and self-proclaimed Emperor, d. 388
Priscus Attalus - Puppet Emperor installed by Alaric, died shortly after 416
Sarus - Roman General d. 413
Stilicho - General and guardian of Honorius, half Vandal, d. 408
Theodosius I - Eastern Emperor, d. 395
Valentinian II - Gratian's brother and co-Western Emperor, d. 392

1. See page 75ff
2. Page 12ff

CHAPTER 4

THE DISINTEGRATION OF THE ROMAN EMPIRE

The half millennium from the end of the 1st century BC to the beginning of the 5th century AD, and the withdrawal of Roman military support to Britain, witnessed almost unimaginable changes to the lives of its inhabitants. These clearly included those who lived in the Reading area. For over four centuries, these peoples had raised families, had worked, enjoyed good times and suffered tragedies, personal and social, but all under of the rule of the *Pax Romana.* However, within a few years, at the turn of the fifth and sixth centuries, this political and social framework was to vanish. It has been argued that elements of the 'old' persisted through the 5th and 6th centuries, though in reality this was as much in legend, and aspiration, as in reality.

To see how these changes impacted on Calleva Atrebatum, its *civitas,* its inhabitants and the development of the settlement we know as Reading, it is necessary to place them within the context of the dramatic events at the core of the Empire.

The date 410 AD is frequently given as the key year when Rome abandoned Britain. As ever, a degree of caution is required when using such categorical statements. The story of the collapse of Roman central authority over its territories is complicated and the subject of much academic research and debate. Nevertheless, there can be no doubt that by the late 4th century the Empire was in a state of disintegration.

One of the major factors was the mass migration of peoples, and their armies, across the imperial borders, into the very heart of the Empire. The map illustrates some of the paths of the many migratory movements during the 4th and 5th centuries.

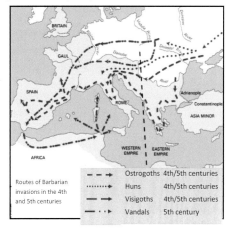

The leaders of the various groups made, and broke, pacts one with another, and also with the imperial authorities. In many cases the soldiers of one or another of the invading forces were engaged to fight alongside the imperial troops. Moreover the Empire itself was divided and frequently at odds with itself.

It was not as if the fault lines within the Empire had not been identified. The Diocletian reforms, of nearly one hundred years earlier, had attempted to address the endemic problems of both internal divisions and external military threats. It was these latter that gave several military commanders the excuse they needed to enhance their own positions of authority, some even aspiring to the office of Emperor itself.[1]

The Withdrawal of Roman Troops from Britain

Before we can look at how Reading developed in the 5th and 6th centuries, it is necessary to understand how and why Britain found itself relying on its own resources to defend its territory. This was not the result of a 'one off' imperial decision; it was not planned from the centre. Rather, it was the result of political and military actions over a lengthy period, of at least half a century, relating to events as far away as Spain, North Africa, Egypt and Constantinople, let alone Rome itself.

Nevertheless, the result was that towns such as Calleva could no longer rely on imperial troops for their defence. In many cases, for example Deva and Eboracum, (Chester and York), the settlements were able to continue, albeit in a new form. Calleva, however, did not survive. How Reading came to replace it will be the story we shall turn to after seeing how and why Rome 'abandoned' Britain.

The First Withdrawal of Roman Troops from Britain: 383-388

One commander who aspired to the Purple was Magnus Maximus. Although the sources are not altogether reliable, it would appear that Maximus had been tasked by the Emperor Gratian to command the imperial troops in Britain against the incursions of the Picts and Scots. However, in 383 he led a military revolt against the Emperor, and made a bid for imperial power.[2]

---

1. Until Diocletian (c. 240-311 AD) the title used by the Roman emperors was *Princeps* ('Principal' or 'Leader'). This was to maintain the Republican element, many would say myth, for imperial legitimacy by claiming to be *first* among the free citizens. The title *imperator* (commander), from which we derive the term *emperor*, referred to the emperor's role as head of the military. Following Diocletian's reforms any pretence of republicanism was dropped, and subsequent emperors used the formula *Imperator Caesar NN. Pius Felix (Invictus) Augustus*. 'Commander Caesar *name* the Great and Good, Fortunate -*happy*, (Invincible) Augustus'.
2. Osorius, writing of Magnus Maximus, described him as *vir quidem strenuus et probus atque Augusto dignus nisi contra sacramenti fidem per tyrannidem emersisset.* ('Maximus a strong and upright man who would have been worthy of the office of Augustus *(Emperor)* if he had not seized it against his solemn oath'). Osorius Bk VII 34:9

It seems that Maximus crossed to Gaul to establish his claim, but returned to Britain in 384, once more to repel the Picts and Scots. A possible piece of corroborative documentary evidence may be found in the *Gallic Chronicle* of 452, when referring to the year 383. It records that *Maximus tyrannus in Britannia a militibus constituitur,* (Maximus was made 'commander' by his troops in Britain), and that the next year *Incursantes Pictos et Scottos Maximus tyrannus strenue superavit* (Maximus the commander vigorously defeated the invading Picts and Scots).[1]

It would seem that the military became increasingly unhappy about the Emperor, Gratian, and his readiness to promote non-imperial soldiers over long-serving regular legionaries. Consequently, they proclaimed Maximus as Emperor of the Western Empire. He crossed into Gaul with considerable numbers of his British troops. There he met with Gratian in battle near modern Paris. Gratian was defeated and killed after his troops deserted to Maximus. This left the young Valentinian II, Gratian's half brother, who had also been his co-Emperor, as the sole Western Emperor. Maximus marched south to Italy to claim the imperial crown. The Eastern Emperor, Theodosius, sent Flavius Bauto with a powerful force to stop him. Negotiations followed in 384; these included the intervention of Ambrose, Bishop of Milan.

The result was an accord with Valentinian II and Theodosius I, in which Maximus was recognized as co-Emperor, that is Augustus, of the Western Empire along with Valentinian. Maximus made his capital at *Augusta Treverorum*, (Trèves, Trier), on the Rhine frontier, in Gaul, and ruled Britain, Gaul, Spain and Africa. He still entertained imperial ambitions, but, following a failed second attempt to oust Valentinian II, Maximus was captured and executed by Theodosius in 388.

The importance of these events to Britain, and Reading, is that the withdrawal of so many battle-hardened troops from Britain, to fight alongside Maximus in Gaul and Italy, left the British defences weakened. It is likely that the Picts and the Scots continued their campaigns. Perhaps Maximus believed he had left Britain with sufficient forces to withstand the invaders whom he had so successfully contained prior to his campaign in Gaul.[2] His death, in 388, marked a return of Britannia to the control of the Western Emperor, Valentinian II.

1. *Chronica Gallica 452.* The reliability, and even authenticity, of the Chronicle is a subject of academic debate. It is worth making reference to it, but the serious student of this period should undertake more searching enquiries. Contemporary, or near contemporary, sources include, among others, GIldas, Osorio, Bede, Claudian, the *Notitia Dignitatum*, (cf Appendix D), and Ammianus Marcellinus as well as the *Chronica Gallica*.
2. Frere, S. *Britannia* Ch 17. Frere cites the hoard of coins at Corbridge as evidence of continued occupation of Hadrian's Wall at this time.

It appears, though, that Valentinian did little to help the British in their resistance to Pict, Scot and Irish incursions and it was only with his death in 392, when Theodosius, the Eastern Emperor, also took command of the West, that the Empire sought to give military aid to Britain.[1]

Reliant, as we are, upon sources that become ever more partisan, it would seem that the Emperor Theodosius sent his lieutenant, Stilicho, to bolster the resistance to the various groups threatening Britain. Such was Theodosius's confidence in his general that he made him guardian of his son Honorius, heir to the imperial crown. Consequently, when Theodosius died, in 395, Stilicho became regent of the Empire. Whether Stilicho himself came to Britain, or, more probably, commanded the operation from abroad, it seems that security had been largely established by 399 and that Britain was re-integrated within the overall military structure of the Empire. Some evidence for the pacification of Britain is to be found in Claudian's writings. He makes two references to Britain at this time.

The first is in *In Eutropium* (Against Eutropius), written early in 399. Referring to events in 398, we read that *the Saxon had been conquered, the Ocean made peaceful, the Pict broken and so Britain made safe.*[2] In even more eulogistic, poetic tones, Stilicho is mentioned as coming to the rescue of Britain when it looked as if it was about to be overrun by the Picts, Scots, and Saxons.[3]

Me quoque vicinis pereuntem gentibus ... munivit Stilicho,	*Moreover ... Stilicho strengthened me when I was about to be overrun by invading peoples from near lying lands*
totam cum Scotus Ibernen movit et infesto spumavit remige Tethys.	*when the Scots stirred up the whole of Ireland and the ocean foamed with menacing oars.*
Illius effectum curis, ne tela timerem Scottica, ne Pictum tremerem,	*Because of his (Stilicho's) protection I fear neither the schemes of the Scot nor tremble before the Pict,*
ne litore toto prospicerem dubiis venturum Saxona ventis[3]	*nor do I look towards the shoreline in fear of approaching Saxons carried by hostile winds.*

---

1. One of the main sources for this period is the poet Claudius Claudianus (Claudian c.370-c.430). Among his writings are three that specifically mention Britain, *In Eutropium*, *De consulatu Stilichonis* and *De bello Gothico*. He is also the main source for much of our knowledge about Stilicho, Alaric and the Sack of Rome in 410. Other sources include the *Notitia Dignitatum*, Zosimus, *Historia Nova* and Procopius, *History of the Wars*.

2. Claudian *In Eutropium*, 1, 392-3: *domito quod Saxone, Tethys Mitior, aut fracto, secura Britannia, Picto.* (Punctuation inserted)

3. Claudian *De consulatu Stilichonis*, 2, 250-5

Stilicho and the second withdrawal of Roman troops, 401-402

Events throughout the rest of the Empire would not allow even this uneasy *status quo* to prevail. Following Theodosius' death, (395), Stilicho was embroiled in a power struggle spanning the Western Empire, involving shifting alliances between the Eastern and the Western Empire, between various Goth and Vandal armies and other armed forces, such as the Alans and the Huns. Even at the time that Claudian was reporting his apparent successes in Britain, Stilicho was subduing the revolt by the Roman General Gildo in 398, in the Province of Africa, against the Emperor Honorius.

But what became the most pressing concern was the containment of Alaric, leader of the Visigoths. Around 401, Alaric had surrounded Honorius' troops at Mediolanum, (Milan). Stilicho came to the Emperor's rescue and defeated Alaric at the battle of Pollentia. However, he failed to drive home the advantage and the Visigoth forces, under Alaric, remained a threat.

As the following excerpt from Claudian says, Stilicho called upon yet more troops from Britain.

Venit et extremis legio praetenta Britannis
Quae Scotto dat frena truci ferroque notatas
perlegit exanimes Picto moriente figuras.[1]

And there came the legion which guards the furthest Britons, the legion that curbs the savage Scot and looks on the soulless patterns tattooed on the dying Picts

It is necessary to be cautious about the interpretation of these verses. Rather than seeing an account of an actual complete withdrawal of a legion from Britain, it could be that Claudian is merely indicating that Stilicho had the authority to call upon troops throughout the Empire, even from its furthest reaches.

Nevertheless, whichever conclusion is reached as to its exact meaning, there can be little doubt that Rome's military presence in Britain was reduced yet further at this point. Whatever the identity of the legion, or forces, called to reinforce Stilicho's army, it is clear that once again British defences were being depleted. Frere is of the opinion that at this point Britain was left with no effective defence, and that it was by way of compensation that a small field army under a *comes Britanniarum* was created.[2] Indeed the *Notitia dignitatum* lists regiments

---

1. Claudian *De bello Gothico, v.* 416-418.   It has been argued that this referred to Legio XX *Valeria Victrix* .

2. Frere, s. *Britannia Ch 17 p 409. Comes Britanniarum - Count of the Britons.* The title *Comes* was bestowed on imperial officials in the army and civil service. From the time of Constantine (early 4th c.) the *Counts of Provinces* were the official representatives of the Emperor.

that had previously been stationed in Britain but were now to be found, not just in mainland Europe, but in the eastern reaches of the Empire such as Egypt.[1] It would seem that, by the middle of the first decade of the 5th century, Britain had not merely lost its imperial legions but also many of its own native men of fighting age, so further weakening its ability to defend itself.

Constantine III and the Third Withdrawal of Roman Troops 407 - 408

These reinforcements did not, however, halt the advances of the Visigoths and other groups, generally referred to as barbarians. Stilicho saw that the overstretched Western Roman army not only had to contend with increasing pressure along its eastern Rhine borders, but was struggling to maintain control within its own core territory of the Prefecture of Italy.

In an example of changing affiliations, Stilicho now proposed that Alaric should support Honorius in his claim to the Prefecture of Illyricum, detaching it from the control of the Eastern Emperor in Constantinople. He suggested that Alaric and the Visigoths would be given the status of *foederati* within the Western Empire.[2] Stilicho's military reputation had suffered following his retreat from the Rhineland, but this pact with Alaric at least appeared to show that by 407 he had found a solution to securing the Prefecture of Italy and promoting the Western Empire's claims to the Prefecture of Illyricum.

If these troop withdrawals were not already placing Britain in a potentially catastrophic position, the events of 406, and the following years, were to have

---

1. See Appendix D, page 122, for more detail about the *Notitia Dignitatum*

2. *Foederati*. The term was first used under the Roman Republic and referred to tribes or armies who, though not Roman citizens, were nevertheless tied by treaty (*foedus*) to provide military support to Rome in exchange for land, payment and other agreed benefits.

permanent consequences for Britain's defences. The continued threat from beyond the Rhine, and from seaborne Saxon invaders, alarmed the officials, and no doubt the populace, of the Roman towns and army in Britain. Having already lost so many of their troops, Zosimus records, the Diocese of Britain[1] revolted against the last vestiges of Roman authority, and appointed one of their own generals, Constantine III, as overall leader in 407.[2]

Constantine believed that the best form of defence was attack. He feared an invasion of Britain from the Teutonic armies crossing the Rhine. He decided to move quickly, cross the Channel and head off any such invasion. In the meantime Stilicho's troops had withdrawn into Italy. For Constantine this was further corroboration that no help would be forthcoming from this quarter. Constantine's campaign was so successful that by 408 he had secured the Rhineland, had won control of Spain, appointed himself Emperor and set up his capital at Arles.[3]

The Year 410 AD

Stilicho (Monza Cathedral)

In 408 the Eastern Emperor Arcadius, son of Theodosius, died. This eased the tensions between the two parts of the Empire. Not only was Stilicho already losing influence at court, having failed to prevent the Rhineland incursions, but the settlement of Alaric's Visigoths in the southern part of the Province of Illyricum was unpopular, with many apprehensive of its consequences.

These fears appeared to be well-founded when Alaric demanded a compensation payment of 4,000 pounds of gold as the cost of standing down his forces, following the decision by the Western Empire to cancel the occupation of Illyricum. Under strong pressure from Stilicho, the Roman Senate consented to its payment.

Unease about Stilicho's policies and over Alaric's intentions increased among the legions. His failure to defend the Rhineland and

---

1. A Diocese was an administrative unit of the Empire. See map on page 124.

2. Zosimus VI, 5

3. This was a strongly symbolic move by Constantine III. Constantine I had favoured Arles; his son Constantine II had been born there. In declaring Arles as his capital and proclaiming himself Western Emperor with this as his capital, Constantine III was making a powerful statement. It should be noted that Constantine III was not related to his namesakes. No doubt there was kudos associated with the name

deal with Constantine, together with rumours that he was planning a *coup d'état,* and to place his own son on the throne of the Eastern Empire, following Arcadius' death, all contributed to his downfall. In addition, there was a mutiny of the western imperial troops, in Ticinum (Pavia). One historian has observed that these events *have every appearance of a thoroughly co-ordinated coup d'état organized by Stilicho's political opponents.*[1]

Stilicho's downfall was swift. He retired to Ravenna and despite assurances to the contrary from Honorius, he was arrested and executed.[2]

Consequent to this, the general, Sarus, possibly because Honorius would not promote him to replace Stilicho, abandoned Ravenna. This left Honorius without any meaningful military force. To make matters worse, the wives and children of Gothic *foederati* throughout Italy were slain by local Romans. Some estimates claim that, consequently, as many as 30,000 men, enraged by this atrocity, joined Alaric's forces. Alaric now crossed from Illyricum into Italy and occupied central Italy.[3]

Honorius had therefore lost his two best generals, Stilicho and Sarus. With no protective military shield, and with Alaric moving with impunity throughout Italy, Honorius had little choice but to accept Constantine's demands, recognising him as joint Emperor. Honorius' hopes that this alliance would bolster his position were short-lived. Constantine was facing his own problems, as the Teutonic tribes overran the Rhineland defences and reached the Pyrenees.

At this point Constantine also faced a rebellion within his own ranks. His general, Gerontius, declared himself Commander in Hispania and appointed a relative, Maximus, as Emperor. Fearing an impending attack by Gerontius, Constantine marched on Ravenna in a bid to replace Honorius and to boost his forces with new troops. Defeat forced Constantine back to Gaul, but now with a depleted army, to await Gerontius' onslaught. In the meantime, Honorius sent another general, Constantius, (later Emperor Constantius III and successor to Honorius), to Arles. The latter defeated Gerontius. He then laid siege to Constantine, who finally surrendered on the understanding that he would be granted amnesty. Constantius, however, had Constantine beheaded on their way back to Ravenna in late 411.

Constantine's ambitions and his ability to realise them had depended on military success and the support of his soldiers. The *Chronica Gallica* for the 16th year of Honorius' reign, (409 or 410), reports that *the Britains were laid waste by Saxon*

---

1. Matthews, John. *Western Aristocracies and Imperial Court AD 364–425*, p. 281
2. Zosimus Bk V 159-162   See Appendix A, page 117, for this account of Stilicho's death
3. For a graphic account of this see, Gibbon, Edward. *Decline and Fall of the Roman Empire Ch 31*

invasions.[1] The very reason Constantine had given for his expedition to Gaul had been to prevent such incursions. He had taken most of the remaining British garrison across the Channel, hoping, that by attacking the would-be invaders in their bases, he could prevent an invasion of Britain. The strategy had failed, leaving Britain virtually defenceless.

The Sack of Rome, 410 AD

Not only was Britain under threat of attack and defended by a much depleted military presence, but Honorius had now lost all his allies and military support. This set in train a sequence of events that was to lead to two significant events in our story: the Sack of Rome and the *Rescript* of Honorius, both in 410.

The Sack of Rome, in 410 AD, is often identified as a turning point in the history of the Empire. The event has been portrayed as the savage uncivilised barbarians, finally destroying, literally and symbolically, the thousand year civilisation of Rome, and heralding the onset of the 'Dark Ages' of ignorance and superstition.

In fact, the so-called barbarians had become very much part of the fabric of the Empire. For example Stilicho, himself half Vandal, had become Commander of the imperial forces and, as we have seen, guardian to Theodosius' sons.

The attack on Rome of 410 was not a unique, nor an unexpected, development. It followed previous sieges by Alaric. The first was in 408. Following the death of Stilicho and the slaughter of women and children that we saw above, Alaric besieged the city and effectively starved it into submission.

The Senate, powerless to resist, agreed to pay a ransom of 5,000 pounds of gold, 30,000 pounds of silver, 4,000 silken tunics, 3,000 hides dyed scarlet, 3,000 pounds of pepper and to free 40,000 Goth slaves.

The second siege, in 409, followed the failure of negotiations between Honorius and Alaric. The latter had wanted a territory for his people in an area between the Danube and the Gulf of Venice, as well as the title 'Commander of the imperial Army'. Honorius refused both requests; consequently in 409 Alaric again besieged Rome.

The Senate soon agreed to Alaric's terms and a rival emperor, Priscus Attalus, was installed with Visigoth support. In all probability, Alaric was merely using Attalus as a bargaining chip with Honorius to demonstrate his power and force Honorius to give way to his demands. Attalus, though often portrayed as Alaric's

---

1. *Chronica Gallica* CCCCLII, Honorius XVI; *Britanniae Saxonum incursione davastatae*. The use of the plural word 'Britains' for Britain, implies that this is referring to the two British Provinces of Britannia Prima and Britannia Secunda (see map page 56). The ND also refers to the 'BritaIns', see Appendix D, page 122

puppet, was in fact ambitious in his own right. Born a pagan from a wealthy family in the Eastern Empire, he was baptised as an Arian Christian on being proclaimed Emperor. He certainly followed his own agenda, sometimes against Alaric's wishes, as when he tried to negotiate with the Eastern Empire and Heraclian in Carthage, to break the food blockade imposed by Honorius.[1]

Within a few months Alaric had dismissed the puppet emperor and, when he was attacked by Sarus' marauding army, this gave him the excuse, if any were needed, to march on Rome in 410, to establish his dominance in the Italian peninsula.

On this, the third occasion, he did occupy Rome with some force, though the Christian chroniclers record the many instances of Visigoth clemency in sparing both people and places.

In short, this third, and most famous siege, known as the '410 Sack of Rome', was not the first, or only, siege by the Gothic forces of the Empire's, by now symbolic, capital. It was part of a long term power struggle between different factions within the military elite. Into this multifaceted problem, Constantine introduced yet another element. Honorius, as we saw above, had been compelled to accept him as co-Emperor and granted him the title of *magister militum,* (Commander of the Army), the very title to which Sarus and Alaric had aspired.

The Sack of Rome in 410 has been analysed and discussed almost from the time of the event itself. Zosimus reports that *Alaric ... repented of his intention of proceeding against Rome, and sent the bishops of each city, not only as ambassadors, but also to advise the emperor not to suffer so noble a city, which for more than a thousand years had ruled over a great part of the world, to be seized and destroyed by the Barbarians, nor such magnificent edifices to be demolished by hostile flames, but to prefer entering into a peace on some reasonable conditions.*[2]

Zosimus makes much of the fact that Alaric issued an edict that whoever took refuge in the churches of saints, especially in those of Peter and Paul, should receive no injury, which was accordingly observed with great care. On the other hand there can be little doubt that there was some plundering and destruction, but hardly the devastation of popular legend.

---

1. Heraclian had been appointed 'Count' of Africa by Honorius. This was to control the vital grain sources to the Empire. Alaric tried to persuade Attalus and the Senate to depose of Heraclian. Instead Attalus sent an envoy, Constans, to Heraclian in Carthage, to try to persuade him to continue supplying grain to Rome.

2. Zosimus Bk V 171

The Rescript of Honorius, 410 AD

The fact that Constantine III had failed to prevent further incursions by the Teutonic tribes across the Rhine, that the island of Britain was now exposed to attack, with little if any meaningful defence force, along with the turmoil in Italy, was, therefore, the background to the letter, or *Rescript,* sent by Honorius in 410. *The Rescript* to the administrative regions, or cities, (πόλεις-poleis), of Britain, told them to look to their own defences.[1] It would appear that, owing to the ineffectual actions of the Roman officials in Britain, in failing to prevent Germanic-Saxon invasions from the east and Pict-Scot-Irish incursions from the west and north, these officials had been 'overthrown' and replaced with local administrators.

It has been suggested that a group of these pro-Romans appealed to Honorius, and that it was in response to this that the Emperor sent the famous letter, or *Rescript.* It is possible that the phrasing was intended to show that the Emperor was allowing the local administrations of the towns to raise their own militia in order to combat the threat of invasion. Whereas raising independent militia would normally have been considered a treasonable offence, the *Rescript* allowed this to take place.

There are two important factors about the *Rescript.* Firstly, if Zosimus is to be believed, it was addressed 'to the towns' (πόλεις), and not to a governor of the Diocese or to any of the officials, Roman or otherwise. Perhaps this indicates that, despite the details we find in the *Notitia,* by 410, either the Roman central authorities had no idea who the officials were, or none had been nominated and approved by Rome. By addressing the letter to the towns as institutions, Honorius was making his wishes known to as wide a group as possible, and to whomsoever may have been 'in charge'.

Nevertheless it is worth commenting on the fact that the towns of Britain still

---

1. Doubt has been cast both upon the date and the destination of this letter. The only record of its existence is to be found in Zosimus' *New History (Historia Nova.* Ἱστορία Νέα). The most commonly held view puts the date at 410 and states that it was intended for the British towns. Zosimus BK VI 177. *Honorius, having sent letters to the cities of Britain, counselling them to be watchful of their own security, and having rewarded his soldiers with the money sent by Heraclianus, lived with all imaginable ease, since he had acquired the attachment of the soldiers in all places.* The key words are Ὀνωρίου δέ γράμμασι πρός τας ἐν Βρεττανία χρησαμένου πόλεις φυλάττεσθαι παραγγέλλουσι. (*Honorius, having sent letters to the cities of Britain, counselling them to be watchful of their own security, ...)*

considered they should defer to imperial authority, and in response 'Rome' obliged by issuing this decree.

The second important factor to note is that there was not a sudden withdrawal from Britain of Roman legions in 410 AD. All too often the impression is given that 410 marked a sudden recall of troops. As we have seen, this had been a gradual process, and one not always engineered by Rome. As Frere says *almost all effective forces had long ago gone to Italy or Gaul.*[1]

Whether Honorius believed that this was to be a permanent state of affairs is open to debate. He may have considered it a short term expediency allowing, in fact 'instructing', the British to raise their own militia as a temporary measure and that he intended to re-establish central control once the turmoil in Italy had been resolved. The fact remains that Rome never again came to the military aid

Appendix F, page 124, shows a map based upon information in the *Notitia Dignitatum.*

The exact boundaries are approximations, and, in some cases, even whole areas are uncertain. This is especially true for the Diocese of Valentia. Frere completely rejects the proposal that Valentia could have been north of Hadrian's Wall. He argues that it may have been *confined to part of northern England or to north Wales.*[2]

---

1. Frere, S. *Britannia* Ch 17. p. 409.
2. ibid pp242-243   See map on opposite page.

ROMAN BRITANNIA about 410

■ Roman army camps   Iceni Native Briton tribes

The above map shows the possible boundaries of the Roman dioceses of Britannia at the end of the 4th century. These are not known for certain.

of Britain or sought to re-integrate it into the Empire. The 410 *Rescript* does indeed mark a turning point in the history of Britain.

We may never know just how the internal political power struggles within the Roman elite affected the common man and woman in Britain, let alone in Reading. What we can say is that, when the legions moved to Gaul and Italy, these people were already sensing the impending threat of civil breakdown. The collapse of a unifying law, and the absence of a sustaining protective force, ushered in an era of continual struggle and uncertainty that was to last, one might argue, up to the next major invasion and imposition of a strong central authority: the Norman Conquest of 1066.

During this time the very nature of the population which inhabited Britain was to change. Even allowing for the intermingling of peoples during the Roman period, the vast majority could trace their roots to Iron Age inhabitants, possibly of Celtic origin. Over the next six hundred years, waves of new peoples: Saxons, Angles, Jutes, Scandinavians, Danes and Normans, vied with each other for control of the country. Each group brought its own influences, which shaped the language, landscape, regional identities, social and cultural norms, much of which persist to this day.

A new country, England, was forged out of this furnace of invasion and struggle. A new culture, and eventually a new language, evolved, based on a mix of all these influences. A predominant religion, Christianity, emerged, which socially and culturally permeated virtually every aspect of the emerging nation's identity.[1]

The next section looks at how these momentous changes affected the Thames-Kennet valley, and we meet the people who first identified themselves as living in a place called Reading.

---

1. Bede's *Historia ecclesiastica gentis Anglorum*, ("Ecclesiastical History of the English People"), specifically Chapters 10 to 12, gives a fascinating and readable account of the withdrawal of Roman support.

CHAPTER 5

BRITAIN AND READING AFTER 'ROME'

The Immediate Aftermath

The above outline of the turmoil throughout the Roman Empire in the late 4th and early 5th centuries helps unravel some of the questions about what happened to Calleva and the area that was to become Reading.

The archaeological records show that there are signs of Germanic peoples in Calleva from at least the middle of the 4th century. The earliest of these are associated with the Germanic Roman troops and consist of buckles and tags. Some of this material was made in Britain but some originated in Germany.[1]

Moreover, these were not just articles belonging to soldiers. British-made buckles were found in the grave of a woman in Dorchester-on-Thames. The earliest Calleva finds of this type, dating to the late 4th century, are all British made, whereas others are similar to those discovered in a mid 5th century Saxon grave in Reading. There are many other examples of buckles and beads from along the Middle Thames and reaching to Newbury, which show strong Germanic, Saxon, influences.[2]

Even if the first Germanic inhabitants of the Calleva/Reading area were part of the imperial army, the withdrawal of these troops would not have meant that everyone left. Some ex-soldiers and their families would have remained. They would have intermarried with other locals. The area would have had a cosmopolitan feel.

In short, after the *Rescript* of 410, the remaining authorities would have been left to govern an eclectic mix of peoples reflecting the ethnic diversity of the Empire. Most of these 'incomers', though, would have been Germanic, as the archaeology shows. Perhaps some of the military veterans were called upon to fill the depleted manpower in an attempt to stem the Irish incursions from the west. So what do we know of the military structure of sub-Roman Britain?

The *Notitia Dignitatum* lists several military commands for Britain.[3] Among these there were the *dux Britanniarum,* the *comes litoris Saxonici* and the *comes*

---

1. Yorke, Barbara. *Kings and kingdoms of early Anglo-Saxon England. Routledge, 2002.* Confirmation of the use of Anglo-Saxons as *foederati*, or federate troops, has been seen as coming from burials of Anglo-Saxons wearing military equipment of a type issued to late Roman forces.
2. Boon, G. *Silchester, The Roman Town of Calleva* Ch 4
3. *dux Britanniarum* - Commander (Duke) of the British: *comes litoris Saxonici* - Count of the Saxon Shore: *comes Britanniarum* - Count of the British. See Appendix D, page 122.

Britanniarum, and the governors of the five British provinces. As we have seen, the problem is that it is not even possible to be sure where these provincial boundaries lay, nor to know the composition of the remaining legionaries.

There is even some uncertainly about the meaning of the term *Saxon Shore*. It may signify *the coast defended against the Saxons,* or *the coast defended by the Saxons,* or even *the coast settled by the Saxons.*

Likewise, the exact nature of the command is ambiguous. Because of the existence of several forts along the south-east coast, it has frequently been assumed that this was part of a military-style defensive command.[1] However, the *Notitia* is primarily concerned with administrative, not necessarily military, matters. If this is placed alongside the view that the structure of the forts was not compatible with being naval military bases, it is possible that the forts served as bonded warehouses for taxation purposes: for storing taxable commodities.

Whichever interpretation is put on this evidence, it is clear that Germanic, including Saxon, peoples were established in Britain by the late 4th century. This would certainly have been true of those Germanic elements who remained, having once been part of the imperial army. In fact the process of assimilation would most probably have been taking place from the time of the first Roman occupation.

It would also apply to Saxon peoples, be they settlers or unwanted invaders, in the decades before the *Rescript*. The arrival of the Saxons, and other Germanic groups, has frequently been portrayed as happening subsequent to the 'departure' of Roman imperial forces. The evidence presented above shows a more complicated, and longer term involvement between the Roman authorities and these new groups, and that relations were not always antagonistic.[2]

In short, the Thames Valley, including the Reading area, would have been accustomed to hosting a diversity of peoples, not just Germans or Saxons. To what extent they settled in the countryside, away from Calleva, is another matter.[3] Calleva, as a hub on the road system for central-southern Britain, would, therefore, have been very much at the centre of these demographic changes. So what does the archaeology of Calleva tell us about the reaction of the authorities to the above events?

1. The towns listed and shown on the map in the *ND* are: *Othona* (Bradwell), then *Dubris* (Dover), *Lemannis* (Lympne), *Branodunum* (Brancaster), *Gariannum* (Burgh), *Regulbium* (Reculver), *Rutupiae* (Richborough), *Anderida* (Pevensey) and *Portus Adurni* (Portchester).
2. Hills, Catherine. *The Oxford Handbook of Anglo-Saxon Archaeology. Overview: Anglo-Saxon identity.* (2011). Hills points out that identity was local and tribal, possibly underpinned more by common dress than by ethnic origins and so with loyalty to a local identity rather than ethnicity, much like football team loyalty today.
3. Wacher in *The Towns of Roman Britain* says there was *no early Germanic settlement in the area. (p276)*

Defences around Calleva were modified in the 4th century, when gateways were narrowed and some blocked. By the 5th century it would seem that earthworks were being constructed to the north-west of Calleva. There continues to be much discussion about the timing of their construction, let alone, therefore, their *raison d'être*. If they were built as defences against a perceived threat to Calleva, then this was from the direction of Dorchester. An alternative view is that these *are best understood as boundaries,* that they *mark a stage of agreement or equilibrium between the invaders and the Britons.* For example *Grim's Ditch,* and other earthworks to the north-west of Calleva, straddle the main roads leading to the town.[1]

The purpose of this work is not to try to untangle the intricate details of who was defending what, against whom, in the late 4th and early 5th centuries. Rather, the aim is to show that the Middle Thames Valley was the host to a mix of peoples, or maybe even the same genetic peoples, some of whom, after the collapse of central Roman authority, found themselves at odds one with another.

It is here that we see that the events at the heart of the Empire, which we looked at earlier, had very practical consequences for the Reading area. The *Rescript* of 410 gave towns the authority to raise their own militia. It was now their decision how best to defend themselves. What we saw above is that the threat of Pict, Scot and Irish invasion from the west and north was very real. We saw that the Saxon presence was considered, at least in part, to be an aggressive menace, but also that Saxon troops were employed to defend Britain from these other incursions.

What, therefore, is the evidence for non-local Celtic peoples in the Reading area? First of all it is necessary to acknowledge the presence of the descendants of the pre-Roman, possibly Celtic, tribes that occupied the land at the time of the Roman invasion of Britain. These peoples, as we have seen, would have stayed to work the land throughout the previous four hundred years, and no doubt many would have become Romanised and considered themselves part of the Empire.

The existence of one item in particular shows that there was contact with Celts from far further west. The Ogham Stone, now held by Reading Museum, has been variously dated from the 5th to the 7th centuries. The stone itself was found in a well in Calleva and made from north-Berkshire sandstone. It is so called because it bears Ogham writing.

---

1. Frere, S. *Britannia p422*

This was devised in 4th century Ireland and consists of a series of strokes to represent the alphabet. The inscription on this stone is written in Celtic and appears to be a tombstone, possibly to *Ebicatos*. Transliterated, the writing reads: *Ebicatos, son of the kin of ...*[1]

Its importance lies in that this is the most easterly example of Ogham writing to be found in all of Britain. Indeed, if some of the other estimates of the stone's age are correct, then it shows that Calleva continued to be inhabited at a later date than previously believed. It also shows that, whereas there are signs of Germanic settlements to the north and west, there was also an Irish Celtic presence in Calleva at least from the 5th century and possibly much later.

The Ogham Stone. Discovered at Calleva in 1893

The First Saxon Settlers

We know from Claudian that Saxon invaders were a cause of concern towards the end of the 4th century. We have also seen that there is some dispute as to the exact meaning of the term *Saxon Shore* and the purpose of the forts. Popular history tells a story of marauding Saxons who, having been invited by the remnants of British power to help defend the borders against invading Picts, Scots and Irish, turned on their hosts and finally overran much of what was to become England, either killing or driving the remaining Celts ever further westwards.

Much of this narrative is based on Bede and Gildas. The latter's blood-chilling accounts have become the accepted version of events in the popular mind, and are frequently repeated in school textbooks: *For the fire of vengeance, justly kindled by former crimes, spread from sea to sea, fed by the hands of our foes in the east and did not cease until destroying the neighbouring towns and lands, it reached the other side of the island and dipped its red and savage tongue in the western ocean.*[2]

---

1. EBICATOS (MA)QI MUCO (I...) Note the use of the Goidelic Celtic Q (see page 15, note 1).

2. Gildas *De Excidio et conquista britanniae* Ch. 24. *Confouebatur namque ulitionis iustae praecedentium scelerum causa de mari usque ad mare ignis orientali sacrilegorum manu exaggeratus, et finitimas quasque ciuitates agrosque populans non quieuit accensus donec cunctam paene exurens insulae superficiem rubra occidentalem trucique oceanum lingua delambere.* This narrative was popularised by the 19th century historian Professor Edward Augustus, the friend, tutor and finally father-in-law to the great archaeologist, Arthur Evans.

It is here that we read about the 'tyrant' who invited the Saxons into Britain. This is also the era for the source of the Arthurian legend, of that great British leader who attempted to unify the nation and uphold the Christian principles of honour and righteousness against pagan decadence.

But do we know what really happened? To a large extent the answer to this question also helps us discover more about the peoples of Reading in the years after the collapse of Roman rule. The first written records tell a story of Britons abandoned by Rome, threatened from the north and west by pagan tribes of Scots, Picts and Irish, and possibly from the east by Germanic groups variously referred to as Angles, Saxons and Jutes. These latter may, or may not, have been *foederati,* troops, some of which, were initially engaged under treaty to fight for the Britons against the invaders from the north and west.

According to Gildas, the British, under their leader or *tyrant*, decided to invite some Saxons to help in this defence. The name Vortigern, for this leader, does not appear to have been used by Gildas; the first use of this name is found in Bede. Gildas merely refers to him as the *superbus tyrranus,* (the proud ruler).[1] The word *Vortigern* may well come from the Celtic for *great leader*. The narrative states that, by the middle of the century, Vortigern had been overthrown and that the Saxons were strengthening their hold on the land. It would also seem that the Saxons demanded more pay and provisions. Eventually, the British united under two leaders: first Ambrosius Aurelianus and then Arthur. The British proceeded to vanquish the Saxons at Mount Badon, leading to several years of peace. Gildas claims that this was the year of his own birth, making it around 500 AD.[2]

In fact, the location and date of the battle of Mount Badon are unknown. It is assumed to have taken place in the south-west of the country, possibly near Bath, and the postulated dates vary from the mid 5th into the 6th century. It is also where we hear of Arthur as the leader who won this great victory, leading to fifty years of unity and peace. *The twelfth battle was on Mount Badon in which there fell in one day 960 men from one charge by Arthur; and no one struck them down except Arthur himself .[3]*

1. *De Excidio et Conquestu Britanniae* XXIII: *Tum omnes consililiarii una cum superbo tyranno caecantur* (then all the councillors, together with the arrogant usurper, became blind). Some mss do insert the name.
2. The chronology is debatable and mixed with legend. The ASC, Bede and Nennius' *Historia Brittonum,* and others, place Vortigern in the second half of the 6th century. Frere believes that ignorance of the date of Aetius' third consulship led all these early chroniclers to placing *the arrival of the Saxons ... impossibly late.*
3. *Historia Brittonum: Duodecimum fuit bellum in monte Badonis, in quo corruerunt in uno die nongenti sexaginta viri de uno impetu Arthur; et nemo prostravit eos nisi ipse solus.*

Untangling the intricate stories within the various sources, and separating myth from legend, and legend from fact, is an intriguing part of British history. Whatever the actual sequence of events, there are key aspects that indicate the settlement of Germanic peoples in and around Reading, at least from the early 5th century. Before examining local evidence, we shall look at some wider issues linking the sub-Roman world to the Saxon period.

The evidence from linguistics and toponymy

Old English emerged as an insular language particular, approximately, to the part of Britain that was to become known as England and south-east Scotland. Although there are no surviving records from before the late 7th century, the written evidence for Old English indicates a well developed and established language: one that had developed before this date. Traditionally, this has been used as evidence of substantial numbers of Germanic settlers, especially along the eastern shores of Britain.

To what extent the people of Britain, and indeed Reading, would have moved from speaking Latin, or even a Brythonic Celtic tongue, is the subject of academic debate.[1] It may have been a gradual process, likely if the two ethnic groups lived side by side, on more or less equal terms, over a period of time. In this scenario words and grammatical structures may have been 'borrowed' from one language and transferred to the other. On the other hand, a more dramatic 'shift' may have taken place if one of the groups assumed socio-political superiority. These two contact scenarios ('borrowing' and 'shift') seem to be subject to different patterns of 'feature transfer' between languages.

A similar reappraisal of the evidence from place names has recently taken place. This has significant implications for how we regard the name of *Reading* and so its peoples. We shall examine this debate more closely in the next chapter. For the moment, it is sufficient to say that there has been a challenge to the concept that names were either purely Germanic or Latin in origin. As just seen, the exchange and interchange of language is complex and open to nuances in the *borrowing* or *shift* of words and grammar. If we accept that archaeological evidence demonstrates a continuity of 'sub-Roman', possibly Celtic, culture south of the Thames, as found in Silchester, then this would likewise indicate a continuity of the Celtic language, or at least that it continued to exert an influence on the developing, new, English language.[2]

---

1. See page 15, especially footnote 1
2. The Ogham Stone, though in this regard tenuous as a piece of evidence, must be taken into consideration..

Nevertheless, accepting the archaeological evidence that Germanic tribes, such as the Angles and Saxons, did settle along the Thames Valley, what can we say about these peoples? It has been noted that many of their inland settlements, especially those that had been used by the Romans, are on rivers. Certainly, the Saxon shallow-draught, clinker-built, boats made such sites as Dorchester-on-Thames readily accessible. To some extent this is a clue as to the relationship between the sub-Roman inhabitants and the newcomers. Frere considers the likelihood that the first Germanic settlers may have been accepted by the existing town inhabitants.[1] This contrasts with the later Saxons, or *laeti*,[2] who settled outside the towns and who relied on continual replenishment of people from their homelands

The persistence of Silchester as a centre of habitation, well after Roman withdrawal, has been commented upon on several occasions. It would be helpful to place this in a wider, pan-British, context.

The evidence from the town and country - "The Groans of the Britons"

There is sufficient evidence to show that Calleva/Silchester continued to operate as an effective town well into the 5th century and, if the Ogham stone is any indication, possibly to a much later date. Indeed the plea to Aetius in 446 demonstrates that, despite the 410 *Rescript,* a significant element within the ruling classes still felt an appeal to Rome would be heard. Gildas, in *De Excidio Britanniae,* writes about this call on the Roman leader and Consul, Aeties, begging for help to withstand the pagan attacks. It is referred to as the *Groans of the Britons,* from its initial lines *gemitus britannorum.*

> *To Agitius, thrice consul: the groans of the Britons. ... The barbarians drive us to the sea, the sea drives us to the barbarians; between these two means of death, we are either killed or drowned.*[3]

Help, however, was not forthcoming.

---

1. Frere. *Britannia* p 421

2. A term used by the Romans to indicate a barbarian or someone from beyond the imperial lands. The etymology of the word itself is unknown. In Latin it means *happy.* However, it may have a Germanic root meaning *slave.*

3. Gildas *De Excidio Britanniae , 1: 20 Agitio ter consuli, gemitus britannorum. ... Repellunt barbari ad mare, repellit mare ad barbaros; inter haec duo genera funerum aut iugulamur aut mergimur.*
The date of this document is disputed but is based on the theory that the Agitius referred to is the Consul and military leader of the Western Empire, Aetius.

It has been observed that some towns fared better than others, and it has been suggested that these, such as Calleva and Verulamium, continued because of their particular relationship with the surrounding countryside. Large houses in these towns could be converted, at least in part, for agricultural use, such as grain drying and storage. At Verulamium, for instance, a high status mosaic was re-purposed for agricultural use when it was dug through in order to make a corn-drying oven. At Calleva, it has been argued, the lack of large villas in the region suggests that the surrounding farmland was managed from within the town. In addition, the existence of houses inside the town with large courtyards and out-buildings facilitated their conversion to viable, functioning agricultural establishments.[1]

The division between town and country had been regulated during Roman rule, so that the economy of one supported that of the other. The breakdown of a central authority in the 5th century was exacerbated by the arrival of incomers who owed little, if any, allegiance to the British rulers. In some cases these may have once been Germanic *foederati,* in other cases they were *laeti* or invaders. At times these people, and their leaders, were living under treaty with the British; on other occasions they were in a state of outright war with them. This uneasy relationship continued until c.500 AD, possibly following the battle of Badon; said to have brought about the legendary half century of stability and peace.

Another important division within the British population, which separated the majority of the British from the Germanic tribes, was that of religion. Most British were Christian, whilst the Picts, Irish, Scots and Saxons were pagan.[2]

But there was also division between the Christians. The Pelagian heresy was effectively a denial of the Catholic Church's teaching concerning the debilitating effects of original sin on the individual's control of his own destiny. The contrary doctrine, upheld by the Catholic Church, taught that only through God's benevolence, or grace, could an individual achieve salvation. By extension, it taught that man was powerless without God. Pelagius, a Briton who had emigrated and lived in Rome, taught that man could make his own destiny. This doctrine of self-sufficiency appealed to the 'new men' in charge of the towns, especially to the 'rulers' or 'tyrants' who replaced the elected magistrates and councils. Vortigern, for instance, was said to have been a Pelagian.[3]

---

1. Wacher, J *The Towns of Roman Britain* p274. See also page 32 and footnote 4 for fuller discussion.
2. Frere. *Britannia.* 'Christianity became the religion of the people', page 423
3. For a discussion about this see D. K. Broadwell *Was Vortigern a Pelagian?* Vol. 15 (1995)

Whereas Roman administrative authority had vanished, the same cannot be said of the Catholic Church. To a great extent the Church took over much of the administrative apparatus of the Empire. For example, the Pope retained the claim to central authority, derived from the 'divine' authority of the emperors, and conserved in the form of the old imperial title *pontifex maximus*.[1] The Church also adopted the same concept of organisational boundaries from the Empire by dividing their administrative areas into dioceses.

The significance of the Church, both spiritually and politically, can be seen from the influence and importance attributed to St Germanus of Auxerre by his biographer, Constantius of Lyons, and other later chroniclers such as Gildas and Bede. Born into a high ranking imperial family, Germanus became a lawyer, married and was eventually created a duke or *dux* of his Province. He was subsequently chosen as bishop to go to Britain to counter the Pelagian heresy. According to his biographer, he first accomplished this by debate, converting many from Pelagianism to Catholicism, and then, by using his military skills, he defeated a combined forces of Picts and Saxons at the 'Alleluia' battle, c. 429.[2]

This division between the countryside and the town may be one reason for the survival of Calleva well into the 5th century. The Germanic newcomers appear to have settled along river valleys, following their preference for water-borne transport. This may account for the ditches that face to the north-west of Calleva. They may have been demarcation lines, as we saw above, or of course they may have offered some sort of defence from incursions, even if not from full attack.

If we accept this scenario, then it is likely that the area around Reading would have seen Germanic settlement, whilst the countryside around Calleva would have remained British. Whether the sub-Roman local British population in the Reading area would have been killed, integrated or fled to the relative safety of Calleva is unknown. As there is no historical record, and very little archaeological evidence, we are never likely to know for sure.

---

1. *Ponitfex Maximus*. Normally translated as 'the greatest bridgebuilder', the origins and meaning of this title are a subject of debate. By the 6th century the bishops of Rome, the popes, used the title, often with the meaning of the greatest of Christian bishops.

2. According to Constantius, whilst preparing for Easter, Germanus heard that a large raiding party of Picts and Saxons had landed on the coast of north-west Wales. Having baptised many of the Welshmen, he ordered them to spread out and, on his command, to light fires on the surrounding hills. The invaders, hearing the shouts of *alleluia* and, seeing the fires, believed themselves outnumbered and fled. Some commentators doubt that Saxons could have been part of an invading force in this part of the country.

The evidence of famine and pestilence

These twin apocalyptic scourges of humanity were never far from the fears and thoughts of those who lived through the 5th century, and also of those who chronicled them at a later date. Famine and pestilence frequently follow civil breakdown and warfare. As we have seen, after the withdrawal of central Roman authority, and for much of the 5th century, there was continual war, or the threat of it, throughout western Europe, including Britain.

However, contrary to previous opinion, there is little evidence that many towns suffered wholesale slaughter, let alone annihilation, at the hands of invaders. True, there is evidence of conflict, as in the case at Wroxeter, where a man crawled into a hypocaust with his hoard of money, maybe his life's savings. Was he hiding from the ravages of invaders sacking his town? But these examples are few and far between. There is little evidence of mass slaughter, or of battle graves. Some Saxon cemeteries do contain warrior burials but their sparsity and intensity do not warrant the conclusion of wholesale death through warfare.

Moreover, many of the Roman towns were strategically sited, both militarily and commercially. It was not in anyone's interest to destroy or abandon them. Undoubtedly, after 410, many, if not all, suffered a drawn-out period of decay. Calleva was unusual in not being on a river. In some ways this may account for its continuation as a British town, whereas others, such as settlements in and around modern Oxford, and Dorchester, were occupied by Germanic peoples. In the longer term, it may also account for Calleva's demise, to be replaced by a new town, Reading, near the confluence of the Kennet and the Thames.

Another factor, which may account for Calleva's continuation well into the 5th century, is that, once the villa system collapsed, many towns lost this vital link in the food chain. As we have seen, towns such as Calleva and Verulamium were able to compensate for this loss by using the town's open spaces, and spacious house courtyards, as corn processing and storage facilities. Crop failure and famines were not new to the Empire.[1] That Britain suffered from famine is evidenced by the often quoted example of the grain ship from Alexandria during the great famine of the early 6th century. This ship brought much needed relief to the west country but it also left with a replacement cargo of tin: an indication of continuing trade relationships between Britain and the Mediterranean.

---

1. Procopius. *History of the Wars, The Vandalic War Bk 4 XIV*. Procopius notes that the year 536, in the middle of the Vandal Wars, was also a time of catastrophic meteorological disaster, "For the sun gave forth its light without brightness, like the moon, during this whole year".

Famine very often leads to a weakening in the ability of a population to resist disease. That what we may call 'killer diseases', were endemic throughout the ancient world, is well documented. These ranged from smallpox through to bubonic plague, typhoid and cholera. There are few medically reliable descriptions, but in an age where many fatal diseases were an almost daily fact of life, we can be sure that those epidemics that are reported, must have been considered especially noteworthy. We can refer to one such in 443, mentioned by Hydatius, which he says *spread almost throughout the whole world.*[1] A much later account of this famine can be found in the 12th century chronicle of John of Worcester. To a great extent this repeats information in Gildas.[2] We read about *the severe and well-known famine* which afflicted the land and forced the inhabitants *to yield themselves as conquered to the bloodthirsty robbers, in order to have a morsel of food for the renewal of life,* whilst others *continued the fight* from their mountain strongholds.

Diseases, and by inference epidemics, spread more readily in populated areas. Towns are, therefore, more susceptible than the countryside with their smaller concentrations of population. It has been argued that, consequently, there was a reluctance on the part of the Germanic invaders to settle or take over the towns. Even in 4th century Rhineland the expanding Germanic peoples were recorded as viewing towns as *tombs surrounded by nets.*[3]

If the invaders tended to avoid towns, it is equally likely that the indigenous peoples may themselves have sought refuge in the countryside. This would have brought them into contact, and possible conflict, with the invaders. This may account for the stories of a general movement westwards. Silchester may well present us with an example of a town that survived as a functioning unit well into the 5th century, having minimal contact with the Germanic 'invaders', but which succumbed to these other factors, leading to its final demise.[4] The lack of archaeological evidence for mass deaths, be it by famine, pestilence or warfare, may be just that: lack of evidence and no more. Nevertheless, Calleva's remoteness, its non-riparian status, the agricultural facilities offered by its open courtyards and, if the Ogham stone gives us any insight, its connection with western Celtic peoples, all indicate its survival following the first period of famine, pestilence and invasion in the middle of the 5th century.

1. Hydatius. *Chronica minora. v2* "pestilentia quae fere in toto orbe diffusa est". Hydatius, or Idacius, was a bishop born in the Roman Iberian province of Gallaecia and is known for his dealings with Aetius, the same Roman general and consul to whom the *Groans of the Britons* had been addressed.
2. John Of Worcester *Chronicle year 446* and Gildas *De excidio* Chap 20
3. Wacher, J. *The Towns of Roman Britain* p. 416. From Ammianus Marcellinus xvi 2, 12
4. Yorke, Barbara. *Wessex in the Early Middle Ages*

Chapter 6 looks at the Saxon and Viking kingdoms as shown in the following maps.

NORTHUMBRIA
LINDSEY
MERCIA
E Anglia Annexed 730
Essex Annexed 730
KENT
WESSEX
SUSSEX
CORNWALL
Wessex submitted 733-752
730-45

Mercia civil war 757, following Aethelbald's murder
MERCIA
Kent, Offa overlord 764
Sussex Annexed 760
746-64

Lindsey annexed c 780
MERCIA
Kent regains independence 776 (Battle of Otford)
Offa defeats Cynewulf of Wessex, 779
765-80

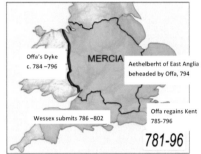

Offa's Dyke c. 784 –796
MERCIA
Aethelberht of East Anglia beheaded by Offa, 794
Wessex submits 786 –802
Offa regains Kent 785-796
781-96

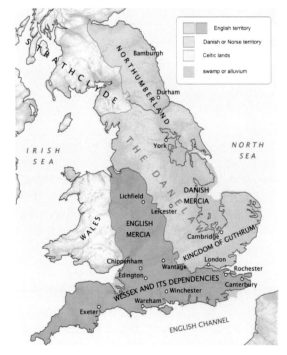

English territory
Danish or Norse territory
Celtic lands
swamp or alluvium

STRATHCLYDE
Bamburgh
NORTHUMBERLAND
Durham
IRISH SEA
York
THE DANELAW
NORTH SEA
Lichfield
Leicester
DANISH MERCIA
WALES
ENGLISH MERCIA
Cambridge
KINGDOM OF GUTHRUM
Chippenham
Wantage
London
Rochester
Edington
WESSEX AND ITS DEPENDENCIES
Canterbury
Exeter
Winchester
Wareham
ENGLISH CHANNEL

ABOVE: c700-c800.
The growth of the Saxon king-dom of Mercia. The word Mercia derives from the Saxon word, *myrce,* meaning 'borders' or 'marches'.

This word itself has connections with the word 'mark' (kingdom) and titles such as 'marquis'.

LEFT: Saxon and Danish Viking lands in the late 9th century

CHAPTER 6

THE ANGLO-SAXONS AND THE DANISH VIKINGS

The National Context

Following the famine and great pestilences of the 550s AD, Calleva all but vanishes and the second great wave of Saxon invasions marks a decisive break in the history of the Roman town, as well as an important period in the development of Reading. We cannot be sure what the population of Reading would have been like. We cannot tell its size, nor its composition. Were the Celtic peoples, or those descended from settlers who pre-dated the Roman invasion, wiped out? Did they flee westwards to meet an unknown fate? Or did they integrate with the new Saxon peoples as they settled along the Thames Valley?

The years following the collapse of the Roman administration, c.410 AD, saw the gradual emergence of Reading as a place of significance. As we have seen, the new Germanic 'invaders' showed a preference for river transport. It has been argued that, consequently, land-based centres such as Calleva diminished in importance.

The deterioration of the Roman road system, and changes to land transport, reflected this new political reality in the Reading area. Calleva, now best referred to as Silchester, was side-lined, as the main north-south road moved to its east. The highway from Winchester, which retained its importance, now went through Basingstoke, by-passing Calleva, then north towards the Thames at Reading. From here branches led east to London, and west to re-join the old Roman road at Speen, near Newbury.

It was during this period that the arterial east-west route, from London to the Bristol Channel, and on to Wales, was established. To the west of London, the route followed the Thames Valley as far as Staines, where the Thames swings north: the Henley Loop. It then cut across the Henley Loop, re-joining the river at Reading, continuing westwards along the Kennet and Avon valleys until reaching the Bristol Channel. This has held true throughout all the subsequent 'transport revolutions', be they toll-roads, canalised rivers, rail or motorway. Reading thus became the transport, and economic, hub that it is today.

The initial impetus was the nature of the topography of the wider area that greeted the Germanic invaders. They were attracted by the rich rolling agricultural lands to the south of the Thames and along this east-west axis. In comparison, the Chilterns, to the north, offered a more challenging terrain.

However, it would be a mistake to look upon the Germanic invaders as a homogenous group. As is well known, the various tribes formed 'kingdoms' and 'sub-kingdoms' which vied with each other for territorial control.[1]

The Thames became a frontier between the kingdoms of Mercia and Wessex. The former gradually increased its hegemony over much of England, spreading out from its heartland of Tamworth and, subsequently, its religious, Christian, capital of Lichfield.

The first four maps on page 70 illustrate the growth and dominance of Mercia from 730 to 796. They also show the importance of the Thames, especially to the west of Reading, in the demarcation of the territorial boundaries between Mercia and Wessex.

The next map shows Wessex coming to dominate the southern and western parts of the country from the 9th century, and how Mercia declined as an independent kingdom following the Danish-Viking invasions.

In fact, to some extent, these invasions helped Wessex to become the dominant power in the south and west of England. In spite of many military reverses, the West Saxons managed to halt the Danish advance, so much so that Alfred the Great, following his victory at Eddington[2] in 878, was able to secure the foundations of Wessex hegemony in the south of England and along the Welsh marches. The Danish leader Guthrum's conversion to Christianity, and his adoption of the name Ethelstan, with Alfred as his godfather, was symbolic of this process.

It was Alfred's grandson Ethelstan II who finally united the two major kingdoms of Mercia and Wessex This set the scene for the uneasy relationship between the Saxons and the Danes for the next hundred years.

In 991 Ethelred the Unready paid the Viking forces, possibly under Olav Tryggvason, 10,000 pounds to keep the peace. This payment, later known as the Danegeld, and at the time referred to as *gafol,* was repeated on several subsequent occassions.[3]

1. Bede's *Historia Ecclesiastica Gentis Anglorum (Ecclesiastical History of the English People)* is probably the best known account of the period.
2. The ASC refers to it as *Eðandune* (Ethandune) and Eddington is commonly accepted as the most likely location.
3. Danegeld. A tribute or payment made to the Danes in exchange for an agreement not to attack Wessex. See J. A. Green, "The Last Century of Danegeld", *The English Historical Review* 96 No. 379 (April 1981:241-258) p. 241. The word *danegeld* is not used until the early 12th century. In the ASC for the entry for 991 AD it is referred to as *gafol* or tribute.

The Local Context

As we saw above, how, and to what extent, Reading grew in the years following the Roman withdrawal, is largely unknown. The written records are sparse. The principal of these sources is the *Anglo-Saxon Chronicle,* and its mention of Reading in the years 870-871, as reproduced in Appendix C. It is also during this period that we encounter our first historical records giving us the name *Reading,* and its emergence as a royal *vil* and a *burgh* with a mint. The toponymy of local place names such as Goring, Sonning, and even of Reading itself, may help in our researches; we shall look at this later. However, with such a paucity of written sources, archaeological evidence is of paramount importance.

The Archaeological Evidence

The Oracle Excavations 1996 -1998

One of the most comprehensive archaeological excavations of a specific area of Reading was carried out under the auspices of Oxford Archaeology, between 1996 and 1998. This consisted of three years fieldwork, followed by post-excavation analysis, drawing on expertise from a wide range of disciplines. The results were published in 2013, in the book *Under the Oracle.*

Although the project, as the title of the book indicates, focused on the area around the Oracle in Reading, the finds, and sometimes lack of them, contribute to our knowledge of Reading as a whole. In order to help our understanding of the scope of the project it is necessary to summarise both the temporal and spatial parameters of the site.

Today the Oracle is a shopping centre covering some twenty two acres. It straddles the canalised River Kennet as it passes through Reading, bordered to the south by Reading's partial ring-road, the Inner Distribution Road (IDR), to the north by the churchyard of St Mary's Minster and Minster Street, to the west by Bridge Street., and, to the east, by London Street and Yield Hall Place.

The original Oracle was constructed in the late 1620s, following the death of a wealthy Reading clothier, John Kendrick, who left the town a generous legacy. Some of the money was gifted to the clothiers of the town to help improve and expand the textile industry in Reading. His will also gave instructions to use part of the money to provide a house *fit and commodious for setting of the poor on work therein, with a fair garden adjoining.*

He stipulated that, should Reading Corporation fail to make such provision, all the money would be forfeit. John's brother, William, also a clothier, who owned property in the Minster Street quarter of the town, agreed to sell this to the Corporation so that they could comply with his brother's wishes. The Corporation agreed to this and, furthermore, bought the related industrial fittings from William. Building work was begun in 1627 and completed in 1628. The Oracle, as it came to be called, provided a workhouse and industrial centre in the heart of Reading which lasted until 1850, by which point it was virtually a ruin and was demolished.[1]

It was expected that any archaeology in this part of Reading would bring to light artefacts and evidence of human settlement spanning several centuries.

In the event, most of the finds date from the post-Reformation period and early industrial era. The question for us, in our quest for information about the origins of the town of Reading, is whether any of the archaeology helps us in tracing the first signs of occupation, and the development of a post-Roman town. It should be noted that, although the excavations were specifically restricted to the Oracle area, they could, by inference, give some indication as to the nature and extent of human activity in Reading generally.

We shall see that the great bulk of the pre-Reformation archaeology dates from the 11th to the 15th centuries. This is clearly well after the first Saxon settlements. If the Oracle excavation is a true reflection of similar, but undiscovered, Saxon-Viking archaeology beneath Reading's streets, then there is very little on which to base a definitive theory of occupation.

There follows an analysis and summary of pottery and other artefacts as reported in *Under the Oracle*. This should help build a picture of human activity, particularly in the Oracle area, but with reference to Reading in general.

---

1. For a detailed look at The Kendrick family and the foundation of the Oracle, see Dils, Joan, *Reading a History*.

Fabrics (Pottery)

Early-mid Saxon hand-built wares AD 450-850 [1]

Some early-mid Saxon pottery had been discovered previously in Reading, mainly in the Abbey quarter, during the 1960s excavations of the waterfront and in Broad Street. The pottery is all of the chaff-tempered variety and is typical of finds along the Thames Valley from London to Lechlade.[2] There is some dispute as to whether the use of the chaff technique in pottery is due to a social construct, or to another wider explanation.[3] What does seem clear is that this is predominantly a southern Anglo-Saxon method and one that is associated with the first centuries of the Germanic settlement, namely from the 5th to 8th centuries. Jervis claims that this is partly associated with the light soils of the Thames Valley. His argument is that, in contemporaneous Saxon settlements in areas of heavier soils, organic tempering is not employed.

There are, therefore, various explanations for organic-tempered pottery of the early Saxon period excavated in Reading. One such theory is that the inhabitants were not fully, or permanently, settled. Organic-tempered pots are lighter to carry, as the firing process leaves more air in the finished article. This is, therefore, a preferred method for peoples on the move.

On the other hand, it may be that, in an area of light soil, organic temper, which tends to bulk out and combine with sandy clay, was better suited to firing than mineral or sand temper. Blinkhorn argues that the choice of temper was a matter of habitus, or tradition, associated with a particular group. In this view there is no need to speculate that the first Saxon settlements were temporary. It should be noted that all the sherds found at the Oracle site are undecorated. This puts them firmly within the early-middle Saxon period.

Is it possible to determine the nature of these early settlements in Reading? Unfortunately, the archaeological evidence is inconclusive. All we can assert is that there are signs of continuous occupation over the whole of the area we call Reading, from the time of the first Germanic invasions. Whether these periods of occupation were transitory or permanent is open to debate.

---

1. Underwood C. *The Pottery* in Hawkes and Fasham 1997, pp 142-161

2. *UO* p 164. *Chaff tempered* describes the process of adding organic material (such as cereal crop chaff) to the potters' clay in order to help control both shrinkage and breakage in the heat of the kiln.

3. For a fuller discussion about Anglo-Saxon pottery and the place of organic tempering in early Anglo-Saxon pottery see : Ben Jervis http://www.academia.edu/1677973/ Making_do_or_making_the_world_Tempering_choices_in_Anglo-Saxon_pottery_manufacture

Late Saxon hand-built wares AD 850-1100

Sherds from the later Saxon period show increasing signs not only of more sophisticated ware but of trade with a wide range of contacts. Two examples of Oxford-ware were discovered on the site. Samples of hand-made shelly ware, in which ground up shells are used to temper the clay, are to be found all along the Thames Valley and are considered to be linked with the sea and the salt trade. Tying this evidence in with the discovery of four sherds of Thetford-type pottery from large storage jars, it is reasonable to speculate that Reading, by the 9th and 10th centuries, was engaged in commerce extending over a wide area.

The largest collection of sherds, sixty-seven in all, is of Cotswold-type ware. Possibly owing to the availability of flint as a temper in the Thames valley, Cotswold ware, tempered with oolitic limestone, is rare in this area. It is possible that the Thames formed the southerly border for use of, or trade in, Cotswold-type. Its existence might indicate that the Oracle site was a trading point, a place of entry into the town. The fact that only two such examples have been found in the rest of the town may lead to the suggestion that the Oracle was such a 'port'. The existence of a single example of Stamford-ware is worthy of comment. This is fine wheel-thrown sandy ware, frequently glazed, and predominantly dates to the late 10th century. Although it was commonly traded throughout the British Isles and London, it is rare in the Thames Valley.

Comment

The above summary of pottery excavated in the Oracle area gives only a tantalising glimpse, and that from just one angle, of Reading in the post-Roman period. The Oracle excavations uncovered little else from this half-millennium period. A few other artefacts dating to the 9th century have been discovered in Reading. One of the most significant was a coffin, containing a hoard of 9th century coins, near St Mary's Minster.

Under the Oracle examines how the sherds came to be in the Oracle area, their possible places of origins, and the trade links which may account for their appearance in Reading. One factor which could explain their presence is the demographic movement, first of the Germanic-Saxon tribes, followed by the Danish-Viking occupations after 870. Add to this the ebb and flow of Saxon re-conquest, doubtless involving not just the Saxon armies, but also their accompanying retinues, and it is easy to picture a scenario where pottery would be brought quite long distances to end up in Reading.

In order to build up a picture of Reading between 500 and 1000 AD, it is necessary to look at a much wider range of evidence.

The Waterfront Excavations 1979-1988[1]

Almost a decade before the Oracle excavations, the waterfront areas of the town were the subject of archaeological examination.[1] Ten sites were identified for research, ranging from Coley Park Farm in the west of Reading to the Abbey Gardens in the east. The time-scale covered was likewise comprehensive, dating from 4000 BC to modern times.[2] In this section we shall be looking at the archaeological results for the immediate post Romano-British period up to the late Saxon times: about the time of the Norman invasion.

The report looks at the excavations in each of ten sites and proceeds to analyse the findings under the following headings:

1. Structural Timbers, Revetments and Dendrochronology

2. Environmental Analyses

3. Human and Animal Bone

4. Leather

5. Pottery

6. Other Finds, which are subdivided as follows: Coins and Tokens; Metalwork (Gold and gold-plated objects, Copper alloy objects, Iron objects, Nails, Slag); Glass; Clay Pipe; Stone; Worked and burnt flint; Ceramic building material; Other fired clay; Mortar and plaster; Textiles; Worked Bone; Worked wood.

There follows a section which looks at the documentary evidence which, by its nature, dates to after the Abbey's foundation. The conclusion takes the form of a 'discussion' which summarises the findings of the report.

By far the greatest record of human activity dates from after the founding of the monastery by Henry I in 1121. We saw above that, in other excavations, there are very few pieces of evidence from the Romano-British period. Although there were more from the Saxon period, these were sparse when compared with material connected to later periods. Human and domesticated animal remains, pottery and other human artefacts are amongst the most reliable indicators, not just of the presence of human settlement, but also of its nature, its density and activities. It should be noted that the great majority of the finds were in the eastern sites such as Abbey Wharf and Crane Wharf.

---

1. *Excavations on Reading Waterfront Sites, (ERW) 1979-1988.* Wessex Archaeology 1997 Report no 5. The project was led by John Hawkes and P.J. Fasham with contributions from experts across a wide range of specialisms. The report is referred to on p 42 in connection with Roman finds.

2. ERW p 8-9. For example, the earliest radiocarbon dating was at Crane Wharf, with a range of 3970-3640 BC

The lack of evidence from other sites does not necessarily prove lack of human activity in these places. There are many reasons why evidence may have been lost, not least the amount of development in Reading, especially over the last two hundred years.

The following chart is a summary of the findings of this report. The figures in the boxes show the number of items in each of four categories; Human remains, Domesticated animal remains, Pottery and Other artefacts. The historic periods are shown in the far left-hand column. Some boxes contain numbers which straddle more than one of the historic periods. This is where the exact dates are uncertain.

Abbreviated record of the various categories of finds during the ERW excavations

The figures below are approximations, compiled from the findings in ERW. They cover all the sites as catalogued in the report. The figures are indicative only. This is because the compilers of the report present different groupings of periods, resulting in overlapping time scales. The lack of human remains is to be expected as there were known burial sites in and around the town, which are not situated on the waterfronts. The most significant feature of this chart, approximate as it may be, is the relative lack of remains dating to the Saxon period.

PERIOD	Human remains	Domesticated animal remains	Pottery	Other artefacts
PRE ROMAN				
ROMANO-BRITISH	3	33	10	3
SAXON		79	26	
12–14th C.		2012		41
14–16th C.		1837	2394	45

As an example of the ERW report I will look at a specific area; Coley Park Farm on the Holy Brook

Along the Holy Brook, to the far west of the town, at Coley Park Farm, (site 10 in the *ERW*), *fragments of unidentified wood which may have formed part of a lathe-turned bowl* were unearthed. Likewise, six sherds of organic tempered pottery, probably dating to the mid-Saxon period, were recovered from the lowest levels of this excavation. A stake, identified as a channel marker, was found at the lowest limit of the excavation, with a radio-carbon dating of 655-760 AD. Just as lack of evidence does not prove 'absence', likewise the existence of a single stake does not necessarily entail that the Holy Brook was a well-used, controlled waterway from mid-Saxon times. Nevertheless, its existence is a strong indicator that this stream was in some use at this time, well before the 12th century Abbey utilised it. What this use may have been can only be a matter of speculation, but fishing (fish ponds) and a designated area for the collection of organic material, such as rushes and reeds, come to mind.

Other Surveys and Excavations

The first scientific survey of the Abbey was carried out by Sir Henry Englefield in 1779. Slade describes this as *the first modern survey* (of the Abbey) *accompanied by accurate plans and elevations.*[1] Over the next two centuries several other surveys and excavations of the ancient Abbey site, and buildings, were carried out. However, all have been hampered by various factors, mainly development and building.

By the end of the 18th century the first prison had been built on much of the eastern section of the Abbey. In 1840 St James' Catholic Church was completed. Along with the priest's house, known as St James' presbytery, this covered much of the northern transept of the Abbey church. Also in the 1840s, the second enlarged prison was built, finally covering what was left of the eastern 14th century Lady Chapel. In the 1870s St James' school building was constructed over the chancel area. To the west of the chancel, the building of Abbots Walk road and houses, along with the creation of the Forbury Gardens, between the 1840s and 1860s, and the construction of the tunnel linking the Forbury and the ruins in 1858, all contributed to making archaeological excavation more problematic. In the 20th century the redevelopment of the land along the Holy Brook, the destruction of much of the Abbey Mill, and the office development at the confluence of the Kennet and the Holy Brook, all added to the problem.[2]

---

1. Slade C *The Town of Reading and its Abbey*. See also Mullaney, J *RAQ* Part 1 Ch 2.
2. RAQ. This book looks at developments in the 'Abbey Quarter' following the dissolution of the Abbey in 1539.

Chapter 6

As we have seen, in some cases building development allowed for archaeological study but much evidence, especially of pre-Abbey Saxon Reading, must have been lost. Nevertheless, several excavations were undertaken and we shall focus on their relevance in contributing to our knowledge of Saxon Reading.

The Abbey Excavations 1971-1975 [1]

As Dr Slade wrote, it was owing to the redevelopment of Reading Gaol in the early 1970s that this *part of the prison area became briefly available for archaeological examination.* Most of the work was done between 1971 and 1973 although *the last work took place on two afternoons of the winter 1974-75.*[2] The excavations were designed to discover as much as possible about the east end of the Abbey church. No feature of this had survived above existing ground level and much of the Abbey floor, and footings, had been damaged or destroyed by the 19th century rebuilding of the gaol.

Plan A

Plan A shows the area of the ancient Abbey in relation to the modern buildings of St James' church, the presbytery and school. It will be seen, that the likely positioning of the high altar was just to the east of the school.

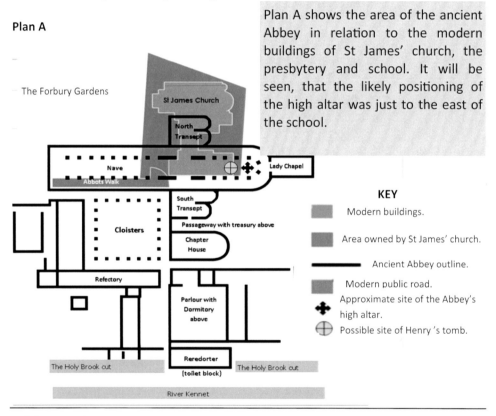

KEY

Modern buildings.

Area owned by St James' church.

Ancient Abbey outline.

Modern public road.

Approximate site of the Abbey's high altar.

Possible site of Henry 's tomb.

1. Slade C. BAJ Vol 68
2. ibid

The dotted area on Plan B shows the section excavated in the 1970s.

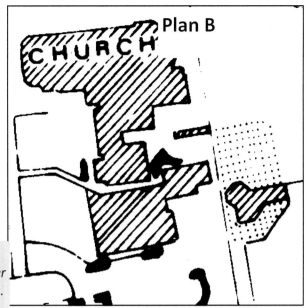

Plan B

CHURCH

Plan C shows the positioning of the High Altar and the *lower footings* as identified by Slade.

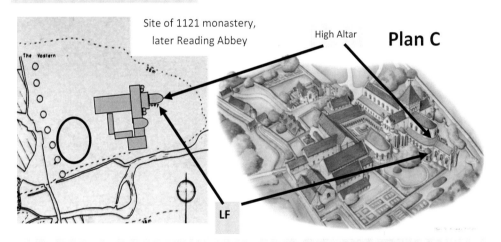

Site of 1121 monastery, later Reading Abbey

High Altar

Plan C

The Vostern

LF

The High Altar's most likely position, and the 'lower footings' (LF) of the pre-1121 building, are marked by arrows.

The significance of the 'lower footings' is examined on the next two pages.
The significance of the oval, and the row of small circles which mark the 'defensive wall', are discussed on page 90.

Plan C. Drawing of the Abbey complex courtesy of John R Mullaney

Extract from Slade's report on the 1970s dig in BAJ 68.

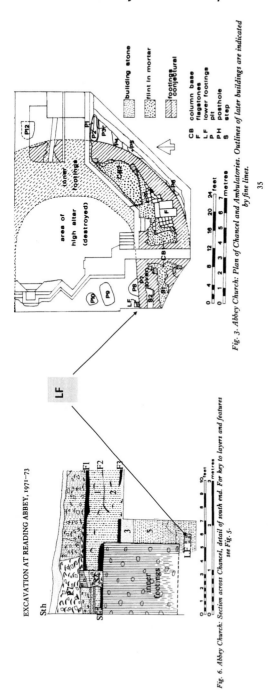

EXCAVATION AT READING ABBEY, 1971–73

Fig. 6. Abbey Church: Section across Chancel, detail of south end. For key to layers and features see Fig. 5.

Fig. 3. Abbey Church: Plan of Chancel and Ambulatories. Outlines of later buildings are indicated by fine lines.

35

1121 Abbey footings total depth 8' (2.43m).

THE *LOWER FOOTINGS* marked **LF**

8" (.2m) below these are pre-1121 footings, 1' 4" (.4m) wide and 6" (.15m) thick, made of flint in hard <u>white</u> mortar.

This contrasts with the <u>yellow</u> mortar of the 1121 monastery buildings.

Imperial measurements as given by Slade in the original text.

It is the discovery of substantial footings, under those of the 1121 monastery, that is most relevant to our search for evidence of Saxon settlement in this part of Reading. The plans are from the BAJ report which show these 'lower footings'. These are marked as LF on the original plan and are indicated by arrows both on the plans and on the illustrations.

It is worth reproducing Slade's own words when describing these lower footings.

In this pale sandy gravel, at an angle to the abbey footings and 8in. below them, was the top of other footings (marked LF on plan and section). These (pl. 13) were 6in. thick and consisted of flint in hard white mortar. They continued under the abbey footings and were at least 1ft 4in. wide. Unfortunately current building operations required the filling-in of this cut as soon as the photograph was completed.[1]

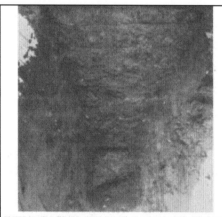

PLATE 13.   *Reading Abbey: Chancel, pre-Abbey footings under Abbey footings*

Before describing the finds made during these excavations, there are several points in Slade's report that require further analysis.

The Abbey footings are generally c.8ft (2.43m) deep. They consist of a core of flint set in yellow mortar. The colour of the mortar is referred to several times in the report.[2] However, the distinguishing feature of the lower footings is that they consist of flint in hard white mortar. It would also seem that at this point the builders of the 1121 monastery used the pre-existing footings as a base for their own foundations. Slade's own analysis of these footings is that they belong to a building of the late-Saxon period and that they were *ecclesiastical in purpose.*[3] The poor-quality photograph of these footings is reproduced here. It will be seen just how restricted the trench was.

Because of the very limited number of sherds discovered he calls this *the first sure, if slight, evidence* of Saxon occupation and he dates them to *possibly somewhere between the fifth and eight centuries.*[4] It is these we shall look at next.

---

1. Slade C. BAJ Vol 68 p44 The photograph referred to is 'plate 13', reproduced above.
2. ibid p34, p39, p40. There are several other references to this. That on page 40 notes that it *consists of yellow mortar that dried off to off-white.*
3. ibid p. 45
4. ibid p. 44

In all, twenty-two sherds dating to the Saxon period were discovered throughout the whole excavation.

Sixteen of these were *in a hard black fabric with fine sand filler, handmade with smoothed internal and external surfaces.* In addition, there were *six sherds in a slightly crumbly black fabric, grass tempered and handmade.* It appears that these two had been reddened by burning after manufacture.[1] Slade comments that both fabrics, the 'hard' and the 'crumbly', are *represented in early Saxon contexts* and are characteristic of the Middle Thames region. To help date the discoveries Slade refers to the work of Berisford and Brown.[2] The former suggests that grass (organic) tempered ware may have persisted as late as the 8th century, whilst Brown argues that its production may be traced to sub-Roman times.[3] Slade's discoveries in the Abbey correspond with those made during the Waterfront and Oracle investigations.

Although this is not a comprehensive account of all pottery finds in the Reading area, it is noticeable that, in this snapshot, the great majority come from the eastern end of the town, specifically in the area in and around the Forbury. As several commentators have pointed out, this may have more to do with the location of the archaeological surveys rather than the nature and spread of Saxon settlement. It could be that other excavations, if they were possible, would unearth similar evidence in the west of Reading. Nevertheless, such a preponderance of early to mid-Saxon pottery must indicate significant human activity in this eastern area. In addition, there is the possible existence of late Saxon footings under the chancel of the 1121 monastery church, which Slade considers to belong to an ecclesiastical building of some importance. It would be reasonable to infer from this evidence that in the Forbury area there was a Saxon settlement, or settlements, from the 5th century, culminating in at least one substantial building by the end of the millennium. Whether this occupation was continuous is open to debate.

Chart of Saxon Fabric (pottery) finds in Reading from the three excavations			
Abbey East End (Slade)	**Waterfront** (ERW)	**Oracle** (*Under the Oracle*)	**TOTAL**
22	26	8	56
	All these were in the Abbey Wharf area	Including 2 shelly-ware samples from the 8th to 11th centuries	

1. ibid p. 61

2. Berrisford, F. *The Anglo-Saxon Pottery* in *Excavations at Shakenoak* Vol III 1972 and Brown and Avery, *The Pottery and other Finds in Saxon Features at Abingdon*: Oxoniensa 37 pp. 66-81

3. See above pp 30-31

Evidence from toponomy [1]

The Place Names

Just as the whereabouts of the first town has been a matter of debate, so too the origins of the name Reading itself have fascinated antiquarians and historians. The name is first attested in pre-Conquest documents; place-names of this period in southern England typically have English origins, but can also be Celtic or Roman, e.g. London. Likewise, Reading's name has been traced by some scholars either to Celtic or to Germanic origins.

In addition to the name of the town, there are several place names in particular which relate to the development of Reading. Among these are *Vastern, Forbury, Portman, Orts* and *Caversham.*

Reading

It has been suggested that the word *Reading* can be traced to pre-Roman times, to possible Celtic origins. One explanation is that Reading is a compound word from *rhyd* meaning a 'ford' and *hen* meaning 'old'.[2] Both these words exist in Welsh today and appear in many Celtic place names. This explanation appears in Doran's history of Reading written in 1835 and is repeated by Wykes.[3] Yet another interpretation is that it derives from *rhyd au ynglyn* meaning *fords that join together* or *rhyd din gun*, that is *the ford of the chieftain.*[4]

These explanations depend on the assumption that the inhabitants of pre-Roman Britain in the Thames Valley spoke a Celtic language. When looking at pre-Roman Calleva, we saw that there is some dispute about both the language and the ethnicity of the Atrebates and other tribes. Overall it would appear that there is compelling evidence for a Celtic-speaking community. This may have included speakers of an earlier Celtic than that of the Belgic Atrebatic tribe. But if we accept that the latter were Celts, then it is not necessary to postulate an early Germanic linguistic influence as argued by Oppenheimer.[5] Even if his hypothesis is accepted, then the above proposition regarding the Brythonic Celtic origins of the word *Reading* is still feasible as, at some point in the late Iron Age, the area was occupied by Celtic-speaking peoples.

1. I am indebted to Professor Françoise Le Saux of the University of Reading for reading through this section and making several suggestions

2. Doran, J. *The History and Antiquities of the Town and Borough of Reading in Berkshire* 1835. p 2

3. Wykes, Alan. *Reading - A Biography.* 1970

4. Bayley, Michael. *Celtic Place Names.* Bayley claims that the Berkshire dialect retained some Celtic influences into the 19th century.

5. Oppenheimer, S. *The Origins of the British* (2006)

Moving to the time of the Roman occupation of Britain, John Leland, writing in 1545, attributed the Roman name *Pontes* to Reading. If true, this may have referred to the many bridges in the town of Reading, rather than just a bridge or bridges over the Thames: the word *pontes* being the plural of the Latin word *pons,* a bridge. We have seen that there was probably a Roman settlement, maybe even a small villa, on the site of Deans Farm and that other farmsteads existed elsewhere on the northern bank of the Thames. Moreover, as we saw, the topography of the area would suggest that this would have been an ideal location for a river crossing, be it a ford or bridge. There is, however, no evidence of a bridge over the Thames during the Roman period.

Leland in his poem *Cygnea cantio, (Swan Song)* describes how a swan recounts his travels from Oxford down-river to where the Thames meets the sea. It is an ode in praise of Henry VIII. When he comes to Reading, Leland writes, *video oppidum, quod olim, si memini satis, vocatum Pontes, Alfridi cecinit trophaea magni.*[1] It should be noted that Staines was also referred to as *Pontes* by the Romans, leading to the speculation that there were at least two bridges over the Thames at that point.

Leaving this digression aside, the first use of the name Reading that I have been able to trace is in the Anglo-Saxon Chronicle (ASC), where *Readingum* appears in the annals of 871-872.[2] Here we find the famous account of the battles between the Saxon forces and the Danish army. The first battle, or more accurately probably a skirmish, at Englefield, was a victory for the Saxons, whereas the second, in Reading itself, saw a Danish victory.

The derivation of the name *Reading,* as written in the ASC, is not as straightforward as it may appear at first sight. The most common explanation is that *ing* may mean *that which belongs to (ing* or *inga* or *ingas)* or *the territory of the followers* of a person called *Read* or some version of this: often given as *Rada.* However, *ing* can also mean a *field.* So it is possible that the original meaning of the whole word may have been *That which belongs to Read (Rada)* or *The field that belongs to Read.* But then there is the question as to the meaning of *Read.* Could this refer to a *red* person, be this their hair colour or, possibly, as has been suggested in the case of William Rufus, to their temperament? We shall return to this in a moment. It should be noted that the spelling of *Reading* has the addition of a suffix *um.* This is an Anglo-Saxon dative plural ending and so presents yet another conundrum as to the meaning of the

---

1. Leland, John. *Cygnea cantio.* 'I saw a town that, if memory serves, was once called Pontes, where a trophy celebrated great Alfred'. John Man writing in *The history and antiquities, ancient and modern, of the borough of Reading* 1816 p 118 gives a fuller analysis of this proposal.

2. See Appendix C, page 121, for a reproduction of the ASC 871

word in the ASC. The 871 entry says *Her cuom se here to Readingum on Westseaxe* ('There came the army to Reading in Wessex'). Should this possibly be rendered *to the Readings,* that is in the plural? It should be noted that *Rad,* or *raed,* may mean a *counsellor, wise man* or *elder.* Consequently this places a new interpretation on the possible original meaning of the word. *Ræd* (counsel) is significant, especially as the *–ing* suffix can also be a variant of *–ung,* found in abstract feminine nouns formed from verbs. *Ræding,* in this case, means 'consultation, counselling', giving us the interpretation of the place name as indicating some sort of judicial function. It should be noted that there are alternative spellings, *raed* or *read* in the ASC and Asser's account.[1] But as the actual sound value of the OE digraphs are a matter of debate, this spelling variation is not very helpful in solving the problem of the meaning of the word.

A totally different explanation can be proffered if we consider that *red* or *rea* means a *flooded* or *overflowing area,* and *ing,* as we have seen, can mean a field or meadow. Hence we could be looking at a description of the town as a place where the meadows flood. Wykes construes this to mean *the meeting of the waters in the meadow* - a fairly accurate description of the confluence of the Kennet and Thames with all their tributaries. Similar explanations were commented on by V L Good who gives the possible derivations as the British word *redin* (a fern) or the Saxon word *rea* .[2]

It is, of course, feasible that the name has several origins. Imagine the scenario where the Celtic Britons called the place *reddin (old ford).* When the first Germanic tribes arrived in the 4th and 5th centuries and met with the indigenous peoples who were still in situ, despite the Roman occupation, they heard this name and, looking at the topology, they adapted it to their own language, called it by their version of what they heard but with a new meaning relating it to the landscape or to the leader and his people that surrounded them. Such a proposal has been made for the name of Leatherhead. Although this may derive from Anglo-Saxon name *Leodridden* ('The place people may ride across the river'), Coates proposes Brythonic origins, namely *led rid* (grey ford).[3]

The theory that place names denote the first settlements of the first Germanic

---

1. Asserius Menevensis *De rebus gestis Aelfredi.* Known as Asser, he was a monk at St David's (Menevensis). Another Chronicle is that of Aethelweard which mentions the same conflict. Written in Latin, it appears to be a translation of the ASC but using other sources no longer extant. It gives details of the Danish army's campaigns (cf Chronicle of Aethelweard. ed A Campbell).

2. Good, V L. *The Most Ancient Church of Reading. 1970* (Reading Library 1211715)

3. Coates, Richard. *Invisible Britons: The view from Linguistics.* Paper circulated in connection with the conference *Britons and Saxons,* 14–16 April. University of Sussex Linguistics and English Language Department.(2004)

arrivals in this country has been challenged. The *inga, ingas* or *ingum* place names such as Reading, Sonning and Goring, though possibly containing personal names in their initial elements, may well refer to the boundary lands between different settlement groups. Doubt has been cast as to whether Reading is the exact site of the first settlement of the Readinga people.[1] In this interpretation the term *inga(s)* refers to the border lands, so that names Readinga (*Readingum*) and *Sonninga* describe the east-west boundary lands between these two groups.

There is a reference to *readingan* in an Anglo-Saxon will made by Aethelfled in 980.[2] Another reference appears in Aethelweard's Chronicle.[3]

In 1006 the ASC once more mentions Reading, and again it is in connection with the marauding Danes. The spelling of the town changes slightly, with the suffix *on*.

> *þa to ðam middan wintran eodan him to heora gearwan feorme ut þuruh Hamtunscire into Bearrucscire to Readingon,*
> 'Then, about midwinter, they (the Danes) went to their ready farm, throughout Hampshire into Berkshire, to Reading.'

In the *Liber Vitae,* c.1025, of Hyde Abbey there is reference to *Readingan*.[4]

The word *Redin* appears on coins dating to the time of Edward the Confessor.[5]

The next extant record of Reading is in the Domesday Book of 1086. There are three entries. The Domesday Book consists of a comparative list of the lands and income before, and during, the time of King Edward, and in 1086. They show the land income appertaining to the Crown and also that of other landowners. Among these is mention of the Abbot of Battle Abbey who is said to *hold a church in Reading*.[6] It goes on to say that at the time of King Edward this was held by the Abbess Leueua (often transcribed as Leveva or Lefeva or Leofeva). Note that the first verb, referring to the Abbot, is in the present tense and is describing the situation in 1086, whereas the Abbess is clearly reported as having held (*tenuit*) it twenty or so years previously, at the time of King Edward.

---

1. Yorke, B, *Wessex in the Early Middle Ages. Pages 812-814*
2. Whitelock, D. Anglo-Saxon Wills *'aet Readingum'*. This comes from an 11th century edition. For more information see Whitleock p138-139. See Appendix E, page 123 for fuller details of Aethelfeld and her will.
3. This is essentially the same account as given in the ASC.
4. *Liber Vitae. Register and Martyrology of New Minster and Hyde Abbey*, ed. W. de Gray Birch (Hampshire Record Society), 1892. This suggests that the place name was declined by some as a weak noun. If so, in this instance, and if dative, Reading is being referred to in the singular.
5. Edward the Confessor: reign 1042-1066. See pages 99-100 for a fuller analysis of this evidence.
6. *Ipse Abb' ten' in Reddinges aecl'am.* ('Ipse Abbas tenet in Reddinges aeclesiam' - 'This Abbot holds a church in Reading'). This refers to the Abbot of Battle Abbey who held lands and a church in Reading. Cf page 103.

We have seen that, in the written records from the Old English and Latin texts, there are several different spellings of Reading. This is not unexpected at a time when spelling was not fixed. In the ASC *Reading* is spelt in two ways, twice with one 'd' and once with two. The lack of fixed spelling may also account for the alternative renditions in Asser's chronicle, where the 'a' and 'e' are inverted.[1]

The Domesday Book refers to the Abbess Lefeva at the time of King Edward, but an Abbot in 1086. The words used are *Ipse Abb' ten' in Reddinges aecl'am*. The Latin word *Ipse* is a demonstrative masculine pronoun and as such refers to the Abbot of Battle Abbey, who has been mentioned previously. Battle Abbey certainly held land in Reading. Most commentators believe that this *church* (*aecl'am* = *aeclesiam*) refers to St Mary's minster (possibly 'monastery'). We shall see that the foundation charter of 1125 refers to Reading as one the three Abbeys which had been 'destroyed on account of their sins'.[2] Even this is problematic, as the insertion of the word *suis,* (their), only appears in one version of the charter. The word used here is 'Radingia'. If Battle Abbey still 'held a church' in 1086, then the questions are: 'what, when and where was the monastery which had been destroyed by 1121?' Perhaps Slade's pre-1121 footings may provide a clue. We shall be examining this in more detail later.

Lastly, in the years before the founding of the 1121 monastery, the Foundation Charter of Battle Abbey makes mention of *Readingas*. However, this is in Latin and is clearly derivative from the earlier Saxon name.

Vastern

There are several possible etymological sources for this word. One is that it comes from an Old English (OE) word. In this view the word is connected with the OE *faestan,* meaning a fortified house, which itself derives from *aern,* a house.[3] This explanation of an older derivation of *vastern* is repeated in several histories of the town. However, we should not ignore another explanation: namely that it comes from a later Middle English (ME) word which itself has Anglo-Norman (AN) connections, especially if we consider that its first attested usage would indicate an Anglo-Norman derivation. In this view, its origins lie in the Medieval Latin *vastum*. The word *vast(e/wast/e* comes from the AN word: *vast(e/gast(e/waste*. It was used in 'Law French' to mean uncultivated land, and appears in Middle English writings from at least 1200 with that meaning.[4]

---

1. Le Saux. The 'inversion' is meaningful only to the extent that it indicates that some dialects privileged a more open sound for the realisation of the digraph.

2. Foundation Charter of Reading Abbey 1125. *tres abbatie in regno Anglie peccatis (suis) exigentibus olim destructe sunt.*

3. See *UO* p5. This is quoted from Astill *Historic Towns in Berkshire* 1978.

4. I am indebted to Phillipa Hardman for pointing out this and the following explanations.

There is also a connected word, used in early ME, *wastine*, borrowed from AN *gastine*, meaning waste or uncultivated land: wilderness. AN spellings include *vastyn, vastine*, which sound a bit closer than the *vast/e* examples noted above. If this is indeed the source, we have to assume that the name *Vastern* is post-Conquest, and it may well reflect land usage. However, there is also quite a rare word that crops up in 14th c. alliterative texts (which tend to be archaic in their vocabulary), *western* meaning *wilderness,* which is a later variant of OE *waesten/waestern*, also meaning wilderness.[1] If this etymological insight into the origins of the word *vastern* presents us with alternative explanations, can we look elsewhere for clues as to its original usage and does this help us understand the origins of the town? Just as there are two main etymological explanations for *vastern,* so there are two potential archaeo-historical explanations. The first comes from the topography of the area. The land shown in Coates' early 19th century map of the 'Vasterns' is low-lying flood plain. At first sight, this would not be suitable for a fortification. The land would have been marshy and liable to flooding. On the other hand, the area does command, on the south bank of the Thames, the approaches to the best crossing point along the river for several miles either up or down stream. In this view it may be that the name originates from Old English, as seen above.

Another explanation is that it refers to the supposed stronghold of the Danes after AD 871. The map on page 81 shows one possible interpretation of the development of the town from early Saxon times to the founding of the 1121 monastery. The oval shaded area to the west of where the 1121 monastery would be built is the site of the possible Danish encampment of 871.[2]

It has been suggested that the earthworks shown by the oval, some of which remained until the middle of the 19th century, were an inner fortification, and that the defensive 'wall' would have stretched along the high ground where today's Market Place, St Laurence's church, and the old Town Hall now stand. This would have extended northwards towards the lower marshy ground, the site of the modern railway station, and so down to the river. It is this area which became known as the Vasterns. In this theory, if one takes *vastern or fastern* as meaning a stronghold, its origins may lie in the supposed Danish fortifications.

We do know that the word was being used in the 13th century to describe the low-lying land between the town and the Thames. In 1233 the Abbot of Reading

1. Cf. *Oxford English Dictionary*, headword: 'western', n.1. As Le Saux points out, these texts also come from a different dialectal area, so the parallel should be handled with care.
2. Kerry C. *A History of the Municipal Church of St Laurence, Reading, 1883.* An alternative opinion is that when Asser refers to *right side of the royal vil* (dextrali parte eiusdem regiae villae) this actually means to the south. As he had just used a perfectly good Latin word for the 'south' *meridian*, this appears to me highly improbable.

Abbey granted to the Franciscans the right to build and live in the Vastern.[1] This legal document clearly confirms both the nature of the land and its location, namely its agricultural use and that it was on the road to Caversham Bridge.

If we look to find comparisons elsewhere, we find that there is a Vastern Manor at Wootton Bassett in Wiltshire. The historical records show that, over time, this has been referred to as *Vasterne, Fasterne, Festern* or the *Gatehouse.* The earliest records for this site date to the 13th century. It would appear that the name was derived from an area of woodland. Around 1229, Alan Basset, (d. 1232-3), was allowed to enclose 3½ acres of his woods at Wootton, which lay within Braydon Forest, together with his wood of Vastern, which lay outside the forest.[2] This has led to some conjecture that this area, and its name, therefore pre-date the 13th century Manor which had adopted the name Vastern. As in the case of its use at Reading, there are no definitive answers to the problem of the name's origin. However, we can say that originally the term appears to be derived from an area beyond settled land, even beyond Braydon Forest.

The Forbury

At first sight, the meaning of this word may appear obvious. Some towns in France, such as Paris and Arras, have a *faubourg.* The usually stated origins of this are that it derives from the Latin *foris, outside* and the Germanic *burg-fortified, town.* There is also an associated explanation, namely that it derives from the Anglo-Saxon *Forburh*, meaning 'vestibule' or 'entrance' to the main town: the way through which entry is made into the town. If this explanation is correct, the earliest town was on the 'Forbury triangle', with its entrance to the east.[3]

Gelling points out that in Old English *Forebury* means an *outwork*. However, in an Old English version of the Book of Exodus, in the Bible, the phrase *ðaes geteldes forebirig* appears.[4] In the Latin version this is translated as *in tabernaculi vestibulo* (at the entrance of the tent). Gelling is of the opinion that, in the case of Reading, it has the former meaning, an *outwork*. In either case, the word

1. *Reading Abbey Cartularies v2 pp207 –208 ... in villa nostra de Redyng' in loco quodam in cultura de Vasterna secus viam regem versus pontem de Kaversham... quod ibidem possint edificare et inhabitare quamdiu fuerint sine proprietate.* ('In our town of Reading in the agricultural area of Vastern, except along the king's highway, towards Caversham Bridge... they may build and live as long as they are without property').
2. Victoria County Histories, Wiltshire Vol 9. parishes Wootton Bassett.
3. Kerry ibid. and Le Saux consider the former of these explanations less likely than an 'Old English' derivation.
4. It should be remembered that 'g' is a modern transliteration of the Anglo-Saxon letter 'yogh' ȝ. The history of the pronunciation of this letter is subject of extensive research. In brief the ȝ symbol represents a sound somewhere between **y** and **g** in modern English. For instance the words ȝha, pronounced 'yea' and ȝhat 'gate', both begin with ȝ. In the case of *Forbirig* this could therefore be written as Forebiry, the 'i' before the 'g' indicating its 'y' sound.

Forbury has the connotation of a place which itself is an *entrance* to another place.[1] The Forbury in Leominster is clearly derived from the 12th century Priory as a dependency of Reading Abbey.

Portman

In the *Cartularies of Reading Abbey* there is a reference to the *Portmanebrok*. This is in a section concerning the customs and services that the Abbot was demanding of the burgesses of the town.[2] It is noted that there is a field with this name, (*cum prato quod vocatur Portmanebrok),* which, along with twelve messuages,[3] belong (*pertinent)* to the Guild. It has been suggested that this indicates some sort of wharf or 'port' associated with the brook that joins the Thames at this point. This would have made it a more valuable piece of real estate than if it were merely a stretch of water-meadow, hence, possibly, its special mention in the Cartulary. Much of this brook was filled in with soil from the Forbury when the foundations for the Assize Courts were being dug in 1861.[4] The word 'port' is itself an early borrowing from the Latin, dating back to before the English period.

Orts

This is most probably from the Middle English word for a scrap or small portion of food. One theory is that the word *ort* means *broken meat,* referring to food that was distributed by the monastery to those waiting for alms outside the Abbey precincts at Blake's Bridge. At the time this was known as *Orts Bridge,* namely the bridge where the people waited for their *orts.*[5]

Caversham

This settlement, or we should say group of settlements, lies opposite Reading on the north bank of the Thames. The first recorded use of the name appears in the Domesday Book of 1086. Here we find *Caueresham* and *Cavesham*. This, its first appearance, is significant as it is somewhat early to find a French place-name or even a name with French elements. We must assume earlier origins.

As in the case of Reading, there is no definitive explanation of the meaning of the word. At the end of the 19th century Dr Stevens, the first curator of Reading Museum, suggested that this was the *ham* or *home* of a person, or group of people, named *Caver*.

---

1 Gelling M. *Place Names of Berkshire*

2. Cartularies of Reading Abbey ed Kemp. Vol 1 no 69 p87. dated 1254.

3. Messuage: a house, its outbuildings and land.

4. RAQ *p.99*

5. Good, V.L. ibid and Wykes, A. *Reading 1970*

Other explanations have been made, such as the possible connection of the word *caver* with its meaning of *calves*. In this case the word *ham* should be taken as having a long vowel sound, making the word *haim* or meadow. This explanation was championed by M T Pearman who pointed out that at Aston in Oxfordshire the marshy land fed by streams were known as *haims*. In this interpretation *Caversham* becomes the *marshy fields,* or *meadows, for grazing young cattle*.

Another theory was proposed by William Wing, who suggested that *caves* or *cavers* means a *hollow,* and *sha* comes from the same root as *sha* or *shaw* meaning a strip of trees. In this view Caversham becomes the *wooded hollow*.[1]

Just as a Celtic root has been proposed for the name of Reading, so too some commentators have seen similar origins for Caversham. Once again we have the suggestion that the Celtic word for a ford, (*res* or *rhyd*), can be found in the middle of the name Caversham or *Caueresham*.[2] *Sarn* is *paved* or *cobbled way* and *cause* means a causeway. In this view we have an etymology which translates as *CAUS RES SARN* or *cobbled (paved) ford causeway*. A variation of this is that the initial word could be *cafell* or *capell,* meaning a chapel. Here Caversham becomes *CAFELL RES SARN,* that is the *cobbled (paved) ford of the sanctuary (chapel)*. When we recall the discovery of the ancient Christian font at Deans Farm, and remember that many early Christian shrines were deliberately placed over ancient pagan Celtic sites, is this yet another possible explanation, or does this seem too far-fetched?

A Royal Vil

The term *Royal Vil* has been used to describe pre-Conquest Reading. Can we tell how important Reading became during the Saxon period? [3]

We have speculated, and brought some evidence to show, that because of its position on the Thames, and at its confluence with the Kennet, Reading must surely have had strategic and commercial significance, at least from sub-Roman times, if not before. Within the boundaries of modern Reading, the archaeological evidence demonstrates continuous settlement in the 'golden triangle', and on the north bank of the Thames since pre-Roman times. However, we have seen that the first historical record is as late as 870. The next is about 100 years later. After that, until the Domesday Book of 1086, the

---

1. Kift, M. *Life in Old Caversham. P114-115.* Mary Kift died some years ago. She was a close personal friend, an outstanding botanist, gardener and local historian. I am indebted to her for the information given here.

2. Domesday Book

3. For instance Asser referred to it as a *villam regiam*.

evidence is scanty. It is important to remember that, if it were not for those two entries, in the ASC for 871-872, and the other brief references, mentioned above, there would be no record of Reading until the end of the first millennium. Historians speculating as to when Reading first evolved with this name, would have to bring the date of certain knowledge of its existence as a place called Reading, or something like it, even further forward.

However, these records do exist, brief and tantalising as they are. In addition there is the archaeology. To what extent can we discern the settlement's importance from these fragments?

It has been argued that the Viking-Danish push westwards was not a haphazard, unplanned raid.[1] Rather, under the leadership of two of the Danes' foremost generals, or 'kings', Bergsack and Halfden,[2] the Danish army planned an all-out onslaught on the Saxon kingdom of Wessex. Earlier raids along the south coast as far west as Exeter, and even as far inland as Winchester, had tested Saxon strength. The move by the Great Heathen Army, in the late 860s and early 870s, to break out of London and drive west, had a very different objective: the defeat and subjugation of the West Saxons under King Ethelred I (Æthelred).

The choice of location for the first military objective, and its timing, are both significant. It would appear that the Danes attacked in the winter or autumn of 870.[3] This was an unexpected season of the year to launch a major attack; campaigning was usually suspended over the winter. However, by capturing not just Reading but also its stores, the Danes would, at a stroke, deprive the Saxons of their first line of defence and of much needed winter supplies.

In the 9th century, October and November were the months when the royal and manorial estates stored their agricultural produce, following harvest, the threshing of grain and the slaughter and salting of livestock. Reading would have held the royal *feorm* (a food storage location), for the area. The Danish attack, therefore, coincided with the maximum stock of provisions.

If, logistically, the seizure of Reading brought the Danes supply benefits, capturing Reading likewise gave them a strategic advantage. Reading's position on the Thames gave them a base to launch attacks on Wallingford and Abingdon. These had long been major fording places and were important royal estates. Reading also opened the route to the Icknield Way by giving the Danish army access to the Kennet, and into the heartland of the Kingdom of Wessex.

---

1. Abels, Richard. *English Logistics and military administration, 871-1066: The Impact of the Viking Wars* .
2. ASC. *Bachsecg & Halfdene þa hęþnan cyningas* (Bagsac and Halfdene the heathen kings).
3. The ASC reports that King Ethelred I died after Easter 871, the next year. This was following the events which are described above, confirming that the Danes first attacked Reading at the end of 870.

It would be reasonable to infer that Reading was a royal *tun,* and, as such, was an administrative centre for the surrounding region. So it is, that when we read the Angle-Saxon Chronicle, we find Reading mentioned as an established and important settlement. How long this had been the case, whether it evolved soon after Silchester was abandoned, or later, it is not possible to be sure for certain.

To what extent it may be labelled a *Royal Vil* is open to debate. If we put together the evidence of habitation from pre-Roman times, of Roman farms both to the east and north of Reading, let alone in the surrounding area, the archaeological traces of Saxon settlement and its significance in the ASC, then there can be little doubt that, by the end of the first millennium, Reading was a place of some importance strategically, commercially and administratively.[1]

Evidence of Saxon Habitation in Reading

We have seen that several researchers believe that the area around St Mary's Minster was the site of a major Saxon settlement. We have already examined the results of the Oracle excavations. Some years later, in 2006, Oxford Archaeology published the results of their watching brief, which entailed the excavation of three trial pits at St Mary's.[2] The conclusions noted that nothing significant pre-dating 1550, was uncovered except one skeleton and some grave-fill material. In 2014 an excavation opposite St Mary's only uncovered a few sherds, dating from c.1080 onwards, and one undated tile.[3]

Likewise, we also saw that the overall archaeological evidence in Reading for the whole Saxon period is sparse and that most Saxon artefacts have been found in the east of the town: in the Forbury and Abbey Wharf areas. We also saw that there is evidence for a Saxon building, of some size, near where St James' church now stands. In fact, if Slade's observations are correct, this is the only archaeological evidence of a significant Saxon or Norman-Saxon building in Reading. As seen above, none such has been found in the area of St Mary's. However, again as frequently noted, this lack of evidence does not prove that there was no such ecclesiastical building in the west of the town, nor that it was not an important settlement.

This leads us to an examination of the evidence concerning the location of Saxon settlements in Reading. We know that there had been a pre-Conquest abbey in Reading; the Domesday Book and the 1125 Foundation Charter refer to its existence. The dispute is about where it lay and what sort of abbey it was.

---

1. Yorke, Barbara. *Wessex in the early middle ages.* Leicester University Press 1995.
2. Oxford Archaeology job no. 3195 *Minster of St Mary the Virgin. Watching brief. 2006*
3. Thames Valley Archaeological Services 2014. *Rear of 7-9 Gun Street.*

Apart from the historical records just mentioned, there is the legend that St Birinus founded a monastery in Reading whilst re-introducing Christianity to the south of England in the 7th century. Another story tells how, in 979, an abbey or monastery for women was founded by Queen Aelfthryth (Elfrida), wife of King Edgar, to expurgate her sin of murdering her stepson, King Edward the Martyr. There is no archaeological or historical evidence to support either of these accounts. The discovery of Saxon artefacts and a hoard of coins has been commented on above. They are certainly not proof of either legend. There is, however, a Saxon doorway in St Mary's, which may indicate a pre-existing building on the site. It is equally possible that it was brought from elsewhere.

The term *minster,* possibly deriving from the word for *monastery,* has been applied to St Mary's in the belief that this is the site of the oldest church in Reading, and so presumably of the Saxon abbey.[1] The argument for this theory centres on the importance of Shaftesbury Abbey in the history of the town.[2] In this account, Queen Aelfthryth's abbey at Reading was destroyed as part of the second great attack by the Danes in 1006.

The Domesday record indicates that a church, if not a monasterry, was rebuilt, for we read that Lefeva, *possessed a church and lands at Reading from King Edward* (the Confessor). By the time of Domesday these had been transferred to the Abbot of Battle Abbey. In fact, it is in the detail of this transfer that we find the strongest argument for placing Aelfthryth's abbey on the site of St Mary's. When Henry I founded his Abbey, the Foundation Charter, (1125), stated that the new monastery should be endowed with the churches and lands of the previous abbey, which, however, by the 1120s had fallen into the hands of laypeople. It is argued that this land and church must be those granted to the Abbot of Battle Abbey and that *none of the Battle lands at Reading can be traced to any parish other than St. Mary's.*[3]

The alternative view is that there was a significant Saxon settlement to the east of the town, in the area of the Forbury, and that this would have been served by a church. In 1901 Dr Hurry wrote: *Reading was a hamlet of thatched wooden houses … grouped around a little Saxon church, which, together with some of the cottages, was doubtless removed in order to make room for the monastery.*[4]

1. Reading Minster of St Mary the Virgin, website and leaflet *History of Reading Minster.*
2. Chandler, John *A Higher Reality*
3. *Historical Notes on the Parish Church of St Mary the Virgin 1914* (Reading Library)
4. Hurry, J. *The History of Reading Abbey* (p26), 1901.

The argument for a pre-existing parish church in this area is most cogently put by Charles Kerry, writing in the 1880s.[1] He identifies several reasons for this theory. First of all it is known that most Saxon churchyards were attached to a church. This custom can be dated to one of the Councils of Cloveshoo in the second half of the 8th century.[2] St Cuthbert, the 11th Archbishop of Canterbury, had received permission for this practice from the Pope.[3] The Christian custom up to this time had followed that of the Romans of burying their dead outside the walls of the town.[4] Now, explicit permission was given to create burial grounds within the towns. Indeed, the Council went further and instructed that this should become the norm.

It is well recorded that the churchyard for St Laurence's church was only moved to its current position by Queen Mary Tudor in 1556-7. We know that St Laurence's was first built at the time of the foundation of the 1121 monastery, and extended to double its size under Abbot Hugh II, between 1189 and 1193. Up to the mid 16th century its churchyard lay to the north of the Abbey church. There must have existed a compelling reason for the newly established monastery to allow the use of this area for the burial of the parishioners of St Laurence. It was not that the Abbey church became the parish church; this latter was the newly constructed St Laurence's.

The conclusion that some historians draw from this state of affairs is that the graveyard lay adjacent to the original parish church, which was removed to make way for the Abbey. Nevertheless, because it was a consecrated burial ground, it would seem that the monks allowed the continued use of the land as the burial place for the parishioners of the newly-built church of St Laurence.[5]

Is there any other evidence to substantiate this view? Could it be that there was a Saxon settlement in this part of the town? Certainly, the archaeological story indicates a significant human presence in this area during the Saxon period. Almost half of the Saxon pottery uncovered in Reading comes from

---

1. Kerry C. *Transactions of the Berkshire Archaeological & Architectural Society : being papers read before the Society during the session, 1880-1.*

2. Probably at the Council held in 747. The location of Cloveshoo has never been positively identified, though it may have been near Rochester.

3. William of Malmesbury (edition Roffensis in the appendix). *Cutbertus archiepiscopus Cant. XI ab Augustino cum Romae videret plures intra civitates sepelire , rogavit Papam ut sibi liceret coemeteria facere (Cuthbert... asked the Pope if he would allow him to make similar cemeteries.)*

4. We have already examined the importance of the Cemetery Junction burial ground.

5. Remains have been uncovered in this area as recently as the 1960s when the north aisle of St James' Church was being built. (St James' Church archives). At the time these were thought to be Saxon, but as no archaeological analysis was made, they may date to a much later period.

here, with most of the other half coming from the eastern waterfront. If Slade's claim about the footings under the Abbey chancel is correct, then there is very clear evidence of a significant ecclesiastical building in this location.[1]

Saxon Burials in Reading

Apart from the many burials in the Abbey area, which we have already commented upon, we have the benefit of having the human remains from the burials at Cemetery Junction, which were discovered in the late 19th century. Its long usage includes evidence of Saxon, including Christian Saxon, interments. Describing the discovery of the cemetery in 1895, Stephens argues that in sub-Roman times it was first used as a pagan Saxon burial place, only to become a Christian one later. He wonders whether at first the pagan custom of placing relics in the grave *had not been totally abandoned.*[2]

In 1906 excavations were made for the purposes of laying a drain between the houses on Abbots Walk and the Forbury Road.[3] The drain passed to the west of St James' church, through the Forbury Gardens, to the road. About forty bodies were discovered in the narrow 3ft wide trench. They were all laid out in an east-west orientation, with their feet toward the east. This was a Christian custom, based on the belief that, on the 'Last Day', the bodies of the dead would rise, and, by facing east, the first sight of the 'risen' would be towards Jerusalem, where Christ would be revealed in glory. No cremations or cinerary urns were found on the site. These latter would have indicated non-Christian funerals.

The whole area lies to the north of the Abbey's north aisle. It was argued, at the time of this discovery, that this supported the opinion, expressed by Kerry *et al.,* that this was compelling evidence for a Saxon church in the area. Ravenscroft suggests that the original Saxon church, possibly made of 'wattle and daub' had been destroyed in the 1006 Viking raid, to be replaced by a more substantial flint building. This could be the one noted by Slade in the 1970s.

As far as I am aware, no DNA analysis has been carried out on any of the human remains found either in the town of Reading or at Cemetery Junction. However, oxygen and strontium isotope data is available for the remains in a Saxon cemetery in Berinsfield in the Upper Thames Valley, near Benson. This sample indicates that only 5% of the Saxon population came from continental Europe

---

1. Slade, C. *Excavation at Reading Abbey 1971-1973* BAJ Vol 68 pages 61 and 65. For details and map of these excavations see pages 81 and 82.

2. Stevens, J. *The Discovery of an Ancient Cemetery in Reading.* (See Cemetery East Reading, p 35, 40-42, 44) See also John Weever, *Antient* (sic) *Funeral Monuments* (London 1767)

3. Ravenscroft, W. *The Discovery of Human Remains in the Forbury, Reading .* BAJ 13 1907

and that over time, there was no change in this pattern except amongst some females. Such samples, small though they are, indicate a stable local population, in other words a permanent settlement.[1]

The Royal Mint at Reading

The series of fortified towns established by Alfred in the 9th century, forming a defensive wall against Danish incursions, resulted in the creation of the *burghs*.[2] These royal fortified towns were given extra status with the addition of mints, so much so that many modern day commentators equate one with the other. There is sound archaeological and historical evidence for the existence of a mint at Reading at the time of Edward the Confessor.

One can but speculate as to the presence of moneyers before this date, but the fact that Reading was a *burgh* may indicate such.

The trail begins with a 1932 work by G C Brooke, who identified two coins as originating in Reading at the time of Ethelred II, the Unready, d.1016 (the moneyer being Aethelstan), and three from the time of Edward the Confessor, d.1066 (with a moneyer named Corff).

This was challenged by Dolley in the 1960s and 1970s. He claimed only one of these coins, from the time of Edward, could be attributed to Reading.[3]

This in turn was questioned by Freeman, writing in the 1980s,[4] who examined a known moneyer, Brihtric, possibly operating in Reading at the same time as Corff. There is some dispute about this, since the Brihtric coin, said to be minted in Reading, had previously been identified as coming from Wallingford. The lettering on the coin was interpreted as *ON ÞELIN* (Welin - i.e. Wallingford). A reappraisal of the coin suggests that the die from which it had been cast had been altered by Brihtric to read *ON REDIN* (Reading), indicating that the moneyer had moved to Reading and reworked his die to reflect this.

---

1. Hughes, Susan S., et al. *"Anglo-Saxon origins investigated by isotopic analysis of burials from Berinsfield, Oxfordshire, UK." Journal of Archaeological Science 42 (2014): 81–92* (See Appendix B: DNA. Page 119)

2. It should be noted that the terms *burgh* and *bury* are in fact the same word and, along with other similar words, such as *burg* and *birig,* all signify a fortified place. As noted earlier, the final *gh* or *g* are modern transliterations of the Middle English letter *yogh* (ȝ). The pronunciation of this shifts from a *y* sound to *g*. Hence the word spelt *burȝ* can be pronounced *bury* or *burg*. The same shift takes place with the word *ȝild* which can be pronounced either as *guild* or *yield*.

3. Dolley, R H M. *A Note on the Anglo-Saxon Mint of Reading*
http://www.britnumsoc.org/publications/Digital%20BNJ/pdfs/1960_BNJ_30_8.pdf

4. Freeman, A. *Reading : Its Status and Standing as a Minor Late Anglo-Saxon Mint.* BAJ 72.

Whether Brihtric was contemporaneous with Corff, or with his predecessor, this would still make Reading a very small mint indeed. London, for instance, could be classified as a 38 moneyer mint, Winchester as 12 and Oxford as 6. It is also clear that the Reading mint was one of a number founded at the beginning of Edward's reign, and that it may have been part of a process to ascertain just how many mints, and of what size, were needed. That its existence appears to have been short-lived, was part of an overall strategy which culminated in the concentration of minting in fewer specific locations.

The evidence for a mint at Reading before the time of Edward is, to say the least, circumstantial. Despite the disputed nature of the coins dating to Edward's reign, there seems little doubt that a mint did exist in Reading, but how many moneyers it supported and how long it lasted are two unknown factors.

There is, therefore, great uncertainty, when we look at the evidence concerning the size of Reading, the make-up of its people and their role in wider Saxon society from the 7th to 11th centuries. Previously, we saw some of the archaeological evidence. The numismatic trail is even more problematic.

Conclusion - Reading in 870 - 1066

All the above evidence points to the long-term existence of a permanent settlement, or maybe settlements, in and around Reading from sub-Roman times. This in itself is far from proof that the same peoples continued to live in the area and assimilated, or were assimilated by, newly arrived immigrant communities. It is quite possible that in the early 6th century the Celtic inhabitants were replaced by the newly arrived Germanic tribes. It is possible that they succumbed to famine or epidemics, or that they were assimilated, in some form or another, and that the two groups became one.

What is clear is that by 870 Reading was a town of some significance, targeted by the Danish Viking army. Over the next 200 years the nature of the town, and its status, are relatively unknown, but the fact that Edward established a mint, albeit small and short lived, in the town, indicates a degree of importance.

The evidence suggests that Reading did boast a monastic establishment of some sort. This is based partly on legend and partly on the possible discovery, in the east of Reading, under the site of the later Abbey, of pre-1121 substantial, probably ecclesiastical, buildings. These may have been just of a church, rather than of a monastery. Evidence of graves, both archaeological and historical, is a very strong indication that there was a substantial Saxon settlement in the Forbury area.

The tradition of an abbey in the west, near to where St Mary's stands, cannot be altogether dismissed, despite the current lack of historical or archaeological evidence. As far as I have been able to ascertain, St Mary's, in the Abbey cartularies, is always referred to as a church, *ecclesia,* and never as an abbey or monastery or 'minster'.

Certainly, there is evidence, from the Domesday Book, that Battle Abbey had a presence in Reading, and it is this aspect of the transition from Saxon to Norman dominance that we shall examine next.

Edward the Confessor - Reading-minted coins according to Freeman. [1]		
Type	Inscription	Transliteration and translation
1. Radiate Small cross type	+EDÞER DREXA	+Edward Rex A(nglorum)
		(Edward King of the English)
	BRIHTRIC ON REDN	Brihtric at Reading
2.	+EDÞER DREXA	+Edward Rex A(nglorum)
	CORFF ONN RÆDII	Corff at Reading
3. Trefoil-quadrilateral type	+ EDÞERD REX	+ Edward Rex
		Edward King)
	EORFF ON READIN	Eorff at Reading (Corff?)
		Corff at Reading

A Trefoil-quadrilateral coin from the reign of Edward the Confessor

1. Freeman, A. *Reading : Its Status and Standing as a Minor Late Anglo-Saxon Mint.* BAJ 72.

Radiate cross type coin

CHAPTER 7

READING UNDER THE NORMANS

The Domesday Book 1086

The main, if not the only, reliable source for the name of Reading in this period is in the Domesday Book of 1086. When looking at the name of *Reading*, we saw that there were three entries for the town in Domesday. As such it is worth quoting, in translation, the three entries in their entirety.[1]

1. READING. *King Edward held it. Then and now it answered for 43 hides. Land for 40 ploughs. In lordship 1: 55 villagers and 30 smallholders with 55 ploughs, 4 mills at 55s; 3 fisheries at 14s 6d; meadow, 150 acres; woodland at 100 pigs; from the pasture 16s 6d. Value before 1066 and later £40; now £48*

2. *In the Borough of Reading the King has 28 sites which pay £4 3s for all customary dues; however their holders pay 100s. Henry de Ferrers has 1 site and ½ virgate of land, in which are 3 acres of meadow. Value 6s. Godric, the Sheriff, held this land for a lodging; therefore Henry holds it. Reinbald, son of bishop Peter, held 1 site there which he transferred to his manor of Earley, Now it is in the King's hands; value 16d*

3. *The Abbot holds a church in Reading himself with 8 hides which belong to it. Abbess Leofeva held it from King Edward. Then it answered 8 hides; now 3 hides. Land for 7 ploughs. In Lordship 1; 9 villagers and 8 smallholders with 5 ploughs. 2 mills at 40s; 2 ½ fisheries at 5s. In Reading 29 dwellings at 28s 8d; meadow, 12 acres; woodland at 5 pigs; from the church £3. Value before 1066 £9; later £8; now £11*

These statistics may be compared with some other settlements in Berkshire [1]

Place	Households (Villagers + Smallholders)	Value
Dorchester	153	£72.
Sonning	66	£60
Reading	102	£51.
Shrivenham	106	£46
Wantage	89	£9
Windsor	26	£20

1.*The Domesday Book Berkshire* Phillimore 1979. See page 88f

There are 223 places in Berkshire mentioned in the Domesday Survey.[1] It will be seen that, by any measure, Reading is among the richest and largest of the places assessed. A look at the majority shows the average number of households to be fewer than that recorded for Reading, being below 50. There are several anomalies, such as Sonning, which, with only 66 households, is valued highly at £60. We shall be looking at Sonning shortly, but its wealth may have much to do with it being a residence of the bishops of Salisbury.

In taxable terms, Reading is the third highest in the county after Dorchester and Sonning, and in population numbers it is again the third after Dorchester and Shrivenham. It should be noted that, although large both in numbers and revenue, at £1 per household value, it is half, or even less, than that of many other places recorded.

When analysing the land ownership, it is clear that Reading was also very rich in the revenue-bearing acreage. The three entries for Reading show a combined total of 51 hides. The usual assessment of a hide is 120 acres, giving Reading a total of 6120 acres. Of these, 43 hides (5160 acres) were owned by the Crown.

With the Conquest, the Norman dynasty acquired a town, Reading, that was already making a very significant contribution to the wealth of the nation. It also lay adjacent to Sonning, a wealthy area in its own right, and a residence of the bishops of Salisbury. Reading was also important because of its location, linking London with Wallingford, Abingdon and Oxford to the north-west, and Winchester, Salisbury and Shaftesbury to the south-west.

The Foundation Charter of Reading Abbey. [2]

The Foundation Charter, as we now have it, is unlikely to have been drawn up for Henry I in 1125, as claimed on the document. As Kemp points out, there are various anomalies in the language used. It also includes signatories who, at the supposed time of issuing the charter, did not hold the offices accredited to them; in fact, some were dead. However, Kemp does not believe these discrepancies give sufficient cause to dismiss the Charter as a forgery. Rather, he calls it an *improved* version, and the main body of the text and its intentions are most probably a true reflection of the original charter issued in 1125.[3]

Does the Charter tell us anything about Reading at the time of the founding of the Abbey? Does it give us any clues as to why Henry chose Reading for his royal mausoleum, and not just his, but that of his dynasty?

---

1. http://opendomesday.org/about/ Extract from data created by a team led by Professor John Palmer and George Slater at the University of Hull.
2. Kemp, B. *The Reading Abbey Cartularies Vol 1* 1986 (Latin), Hurry, J. *Reading Abbey Appendix ii.* 1901.
3. Kemp ibid. p35-36

To answer these questions we will examine the Charter from a different angle than that usually used. But first we shall look at its main provisions.

The Charter begins by noting that Reading's ancient abbey, along with those of Cholsey and Leominster, had been destroyed on account of (their) sins, (*peccatis exigentibus olim destructe sunt*). Henry then tells us why he is founding this new Abbey: namely, for the salvation of his soul and those of all his ancestors and successors, (*omnium antecessorum at successorum meorum*). Interestingly, the Charter also says that, along with the fields, mills, etc, Henry endows Reading with a mint and one moneyer, (*cum moneta et uno monetario apud Radingiam*). There follows a long list of the rights, and duties, of the Abbot and the monks.[1] What is not said is why Henry chose Reading for such an important foundation.

Roger, Bishop of Salisbury c.1125

Two more references that may help us gauge the status of Reading around the time of the Abbey's foundation are both from Roger, Bishop of Salisbury, and make reference to the mint.[2] The first is a general notification of its existence. The second says that the King has given the Abbot and monks of Reading a moneyer, named Edgar, and a mint in London.[3] Presumably this followed on from, or was later than, the original charter, and later also than the first of the Bishop of Salisbury's notifications.

The likely reason for the decision to establish Reading's mint in London can be found in the events of 1124/5. Whilst Henry was campaigning in France and Normandy, it was discovered that the money used to pay his soldiers had been debased. Henry sent orders to Roger, in England, that coin debasers were to be castrated and lose their right hands. The moneyers were summoned to Winchester, where they were mutilated.[4] Subsequently, Henry initiated reforms which involved closing the small mints and centralising the minting of coins, thereby creating a stable and fixed issue. It is possible that the decrees issued by Roger regarding the Reading mint were part of this process.

It should be noted that Roger of Salisbury acted as regent (*procurator*)[5] of England whilst Henry was in Normandy. This relationship had its roots in Henry's youth. We shall be returning later to Roger's importance in Henry's life.

---

1. Kemp ibid. p 33-36
2. The See was at Old Sarum. Today's Salisbury cathedral was built a hundred years later
3. Kemp ibid. Vol 1. p 145 no 177
4. The ASC (ms E) gives the year as 1125 and refers to the *riht hand heora stanen beneðan*, (the right hand, and that which lies beneath). Margan gives the year as 1124 and says around Epiphany, 94 moneyers were thus punished. Hollister notes that coining false money (this was debasing rather than forgery) was punishable by excommunication, as decreed by the Lateran Council of 1123.
5. This is the title Roger applied to himself and which appears at the start of his notification.

Henry and the Status of Reading before 1121

What can be inferred from the above regarding the status of Reading before Henry founded his monastery in 1121?

It was clearly an above average-sized town with a significant value at the time of Domesday. Its proximity to Sonning, the site of the Bishop of Salisbury's palace, must have added to its prestige.

That Henry visited Reading, and knew the town, can be surmised from the record of charters, writs and other edicts issued at Reading in the presence of the King.[1]

The first, in 1102, in the Cartularies of Ramsey, was attested by Queen Matilda, Archbishop Gerard, Bishop of Lincoln, Robert, Count of Meulan, and other barons (*et aliis baronibus*).

A second was a mandate, issued between May 1108 and August 1111 and addressed to the Bishop of Worcester and the sheriff, Urse d'Abetot, which ordered that *the shire and hundred courts be held in those places and at those intervals that they had been at the time of King Edward, and not otherwise.*[2] This was witnessed by Richard Bishop of London, Roger Bishop of Salisbury, Ranulf the Chancellor and Robert Count of Meulan.

It is worth noting that Henry had managed to persuade Anselm, Archbishop of Canterbury, to consecrate his close friend, Roger of Avranches, as Bishop of Salisbury, in August 1107.[3] Henry's connection with the bishops of Salisbury may well go much further back; to his youth. Whereas what we have seen so far is well attested through contemporary documents, a rather more speculative possibility is that Henry was educated for some years at Salisbury, (Old Sarum), at the time of Bishop Osmund (1078-1099). Certainly, the historical records do show that between 1080 and 1086, when Henry was between 12 and 18 years old, he is recorded as being in the Bishop's entourage at Abingdon Abbey.[4]

Osmund's name also appeared on the royal charters which both he and Henry witnessed between the years 1080-1086. Hollister argues that the hypothesis *that Henry was reared at Salisbury is altogether plausible, but altogether circumstantial.* As some of these charters are spurious, care needs to be taken in accepting them all. Nevertheless, there can be little doubt that Henry did spend some time in the company of Osmund and his court whilst a youth. By extension,

1. Farrer, W. *An Outline Itinerary of King Henry the First.* 1919 Farrer records four such visits before 1121.
2. Green, J. *Henry I.* 2009 p115-116. Green shows the reasoning for dating this writ to 1108.
3. According to the *Annales de Margan,* Roger was elected *Bishop of Salisbury* in 1102, but was only consecrated by Anselm in 1107.
4. Abingdon Chronicles 2:2. Also see Warrren Hollister *Henry I p 36-37*

therefore, it would be logical to speculate that Henry may have accompanied the Bishop to his palace at Sonning and so been familiar with Reading.

Thirdly, in 1111, there was a writ addressed to Hugh de Bocheland, the ministers of London and Reiner the reeve. This was attested by Robert, Bishop of Lincoln and John of Bayeux.

A fourth, in 1116, was a notification about an exchange of land near to the church of St Frideswide, Oxford. This was witnessed by the bishops Robert of Lincoln and Hervey of Ely, Ranulf the Chancellor, Robert the King's son, and Ranulf Meschin.

On the occasions when Henry was in Reading with his court, he would have been surrounded by other prestigious figures, with their entourages. There may have been other visits when writs etc were not issued. The indications are that Reading was a town of some significance, which had the facilities to host the Royal Court and all that entailed. This raises the question as to the nature of the buildings which housed the court. Was the 'church' mentioned in Domesday a monastery with sufficient outbuildings to accommodate such a large number of visitors? Some may have pitched camp, but it seems logical to assume the existence of suitable buildings.

This gives us some idea of the Reading and Sonning that Henry would have seen when he came to the area. Is there any way of portraying the Reading that the Cluniac monks would have found when they arrived in 1121?

One clue lies in the chronicle of William of Malmesbury, a contemporary of Henry.[1] He singles out the new monastery at Reading, and in so doing gives us an insight, not just into its early years, but into why Henry chose this town as his great monastery and intended mausoleum. It is worth repeating his words in full.

> *He built this monastery between the rivers Kennet and Thames, in a place calculated for the reception of almost all who might have occasion to travel to the most populous cities in England ... here may be seen what is peculiar to this place: for guests arriving every hour, consume more than the inmates themselves.*[2]

We saw above that the Foundation Charter talks about the spiritual reason for the creation of the Abbey. Here we have a more pragmatic account. Reading's geographical situation, as we have consistently seen throughout our survey, is an ideal location to act as a transport hub for the south of England. Henry himself

---

1. Giles, J.A. *William of Malmesbury's Chronicle.* 1847. The translator, in his preface page vii, places William's birth as between 1084 and 1105.

2. Giles ibid. p 447 . For the Latin version and final comment see page 116

was constantly on the move, and Reading offered a conveniently situated location *en route* for his visits to Winchester, Oxford, Abingdon, Windsor and London, to mention just a few of the places he visited regularly.

Henry was intent both on unifying and on controlling his kingdom. He was, as often as not, in Normandy, but he was not slow to delegate authority to his trusted lieutenants, such as Roger of Salisbury.[1] Indeed, Warren Hollister identifies three 'supermagnates' who helped Henry govern. These were his eldest illegitimate son, Robert of Gloucester, his nephew and the future King, Stephen of Blois, and Roger. Below these Hollister identifies eight 'magnates', and below these again between forty to fifty powerful laymen.[2]

If Reading was to become such a crossroads for the Kingdom, and so a potential meeting place for those who might even oppose Henry, it was surely advantageous that it should be close to the domain of his trusted 'supermagnate', and indeed viceroy, Roger.[3] In fact the monastery and town fell within the jurisdiction of the Bishop of Salisbury, who would therefore be responsible for the regular 'visitations' or examinations of the Abbey.

There can be little doubt that by 1121 Henry was well acquainted with both Sonning and Reading. We have seen that he was in Reading on several occasions, and that this would have been with his court, and so would have comprised a significant number of people. It is possible that some may have lodged at Sonning. Even allowing for a number staying in a pitched camp, there must have been a residence suitable to house, and maintain, the court whilst Henry was at Reading.

Even if Henry himself stayed at Sonning, the fact that these documents are listed as being issued and witnessed at Reading, indicates the existence of at least one appropriate building. The existence, according to Slade, of sizeable footings below the chancel area of the 1121 monastery would confirm the possibility of such a structure in the eastern part of town. There may of course have been others elsewhere, such as at St Mary's.

---

1. According to Haskins in *Norman Institutions,* Henry was in Normandy during the years 1104, 1106-1107, 1108-1109, 1111-1113, 1114-1115, 1116-1120, 1123-1126, 1127-1129, 1130-1131, 1133-1135.
2. Warren Hollsister, *Henry I* Ch 8
3. Henry appointed Roger as his Chancellor in 1101, only one year after his accession to the throne.

CHAPTER 8

READING AND THE ABBEY OF THE VIRGIN MARY
AND ST JOHN THE EVANGELIST

The evidence from Domesday, the existence of a mint, (albeit transitory and small), the town's strategic geographic position, the fact that the Royal Court was present on several occasions between 1100 and 1121, the known existence of a previous abbey and a church in 1086 with some considerable land, and finally, the very fact Henry chose Reading for his main religious foundation, all act to demonstrate the role Reading played in the early years of the 12th century.

Henry was very aware that his new monastery would radically change the town. It is often claimed that the death of his son and heir, William Adelin, in the White Ship disaster, was the immediate cause of its foundation. The likelihood is that he was already thinking about founding an abbey before the tragic events of 1120. Perhaps the death of his son, William, acted as a spur. Moreover, the Foundation Charter, whilst giving several reasons for its foundation, does not specifically give this as a reason. His son, William, is mentioned only in the list of all his other relatives.

Several scholars have puzzled over the words in the *Foundation Charter* which refer to the previous abbeys at Reading and those of Leominster and Cholsey, all of which had been *destroyed on account of (their) sins: 'peccatis (suis) exigentibus olim destructe sunt'*. Some commentators have interpreted this as referring to the Danish attack in 1006 under King Sweyn. Yet the Domesday record states that at the time of King Edward (the Confessor) the Abbess Lefeva had held a church in Reading, and that in 1066 the Abbot of Battle Abbey owned it. The Charter indicates that it no longer existed, and that Henry's monastery was built to replace it.

The evidence of Domesday shows that there was a church with some considerable wealth in Reading. The fact that this was once held by the Abbess Lefeva, raises the question as to whether this was just a church, or whether there was still an active monastery at this time in Reading, or had it indeed been destroyed in 1006 and never replaced? The Foundation Charter says that the lands had passed into the hands of lay people. If, therefore, there was an abbey which had been destroyed, we must ask: what were the 'sins', referred to in the Charter, that caused its destruction?

Kemp, in his commentary about the Cartularies, notes that, in the words *on account of their sins,* the Latin word for *their, (suis),* is omitted in all but one of the manuscripts.[1] Does this alter the meaning? In one sense it removes any particular guilt from these three monasteries, but still attributes some form of general blame or *sin.* We may never know what this was, but looking first at when and how the other two monasteries of Leominster and Cholsey were destroyed, and secondly at the state of the church in the first half of the 12th century, may shed some light on the problem.

It is probable that the monasteries of Reading and Cholsey were partly, or totally, destroyed in 1006. This was the year when the Danes, under King Sweyn, overran this district and burnt Wallingford.[2] They probably also sacked Cholsey Abbey, near to Wallingford, which was founded about 986 by Ethelred II, as an act of expiation for the death of his half-brother, Edward the Martyr.

In the case of Leominster, it would seem as if the destruction referred to may not have been at the hands of the Danes. It has been suggested instead that this was due to the actions of Earl Swein. This is not the King Sweyn mentioned above, but the brother of Harold Godwinson, later King of England, who was defeated at Hastings by Duke William of Normandy. The story goes that, in 1046, Swein dragged the abbess, Eadgifu, from her monastery, held her captive and raped her. The ASC reports for the year 1046:

> *This year went Earl Sweine into Wales; and Griffin*
> *king of the northern men with him; and hostages were delivered to*
> *him. As he returned homeward, he ordered the Abbess of Leominster to be*
> *fetched him; and he had her as long as he list after which he let her go home ...*[3]

Turning to Reading, it has been conjectured that the monastery here was established at the same time as that of Cholsey, by Elfrida, in atonement for her involvement in the death of Edward the Martyr, her stepson. As we have seen, there is no historical evidence for this, but that does not preclude its possibility.

---

1. Kemp, B. *Cartularies Vol 1 p 35*
2. ASC year 1006. *þa to ðam middan wintran eodon heom to heora garwan feorme ut þurh Hamtunscire into Barrucscire to Rædingan.* (Then, about midwinter, they went to their ready farm, throughout Hampshire into Berkshire, to Reading.) Although the ASC does say that Wallingford was destroyed by the Danes, this is not specified for Reading
3. ASC year 1046 *Her on þysum ȝeare for Sweȝn eorl into Wealan, & Griffin se norþerna cynȝ forð mid him, & him man ȝislode. Þa he hamwerdes wæs, þa het e feccan him to þa abbedessan on Leomynstre, & hæfde hi þa while þe him ȝeliste let hi syþþan faran ham.* See page 91 note 4 for ȝ (yogh) sound. The þ = th.

Allowing for the fact that Reading did posses a church, as evidenced in Domesday, can we tell anything more about it, and why it may have been replaced by the Normans? By comparing Reading with other towns, when their monasteries or churches had been destroyed, and where their replacements had been built, the chances are that the Reading church (or churches) would have been rebuilt on the same sacred ground as previously occupied by the former ecclesiastical buildings. We are now presented with the following possibilities.

First, the abbey referred to in the Foundation Charter was one that had been destroyed in the 1006 raid. Subsequent to this a Saxon church was built or rebuilt, or indeed survived despite the abbey being sacked, and this is the one mentioned in Domesday. If this were on the site of St Mary's, then a further complication is that, if the findings of the 1970s excavations on the site of Norman Abbey are correct, we would have to account for two churches, of some significance, in Reading. This is not an impossible scenario and it would indicate that Reading was indeed a sizeable town.

The second possibility is that the earlier abbey mentioned in the Foundation Charter may have been the one that was possibly destroyed in 1006 but this destruction was only partial and a small community returned at a later date. In this case, like the abbey at Leominster, it may have been destroyed some time after.

We do have another clue as to why these abbeys, along with many other religious establishments, monasteries and churches, were destroyed, only to be replaced with new foundations, by the new Norman rulers. Orderic comments on how many Saxon churches were demolished to make way for new Norman ones on the same sites. As part of his eulogy of Henry I, he comments on how peace prevailed in the Kingdom and the Church of God flourished.[1] This, he says: *is evidenced by the number of new churches and chantries recently erected in the villages of England, as well as by the cloistered buildings of the abbeys and other monastic offices constructed during King Henry's reign.* He goes on to comment that: *the faithful undertook to demolish the temples and habitations that they might substitute for them edifices on a better scale. The buildings that were erected at the times of Edgar, Edward and other Christian kings were therefore levelled to the ground that they might be succeeded by others, larger and loftier, and of more elegant architecture, to the Creator's glory.*

---

1. Ordericus Vitalis. *Historia Ecclesiastica* Vol 3 Book 10 Chapter 18. Page 286. Orderic (1075—c. 1142) Orderic was a contemporary of Henry. He was a Benedictine monk and is one of the most reliable, and readable, of the contemporary sources, though somewhat biased in his favourable opinion of Henry.

This was not merely the consequence of a grand building programme. These new buildings may be seen as a religious counterpart to the establishment of castles, the secular symbols of Norman domination.[1]

Even the choice of location of the new monasteries appears to have received special attention. A study in 1986 showed that, of the one hundred and seventy monasteries founded between 1066 and 1300, the great majority were near a castle.[2] That Reading does not appear to have had a castle built after the Conquest, not even a primitive motte and bailey, is a factor that is rarely commented upon. What does this tell us about the status of Reading in the late 11th century, and does it add anything to our understanding of why Henry chose Reading for his new monastery?

The new religious foundations were rebuilt using the impressive Norman architectural style. As already stated, they were, along with castles, a very tangible statement of power and domination by the Norman elite. The lack of a castle at Reading could signify the town's relatively low status, or that the area was not seen as posing a military threat to the new regime. Could it be that Henry, wishing to establish a purely religious symbol, chose Reading for his new monastery precisely because it did not have military connotations?

Apart from the existing grandeur of Edward's Westminster Abbey, which already followed the continental influence, the smaller, 'inadequate', Saxon religious buildings were consciously replaced with this new design, which was intended not just to make a statement of power, but to draw the populace and visitors into these holy spaces. In other words, the regime offered attractive incentives, as well a threats, to the conquered Saxons. Part of this was the stunning, elaborate, liturgy for which the new buildings were designed.

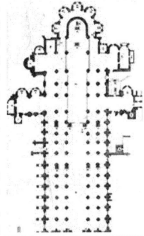

Cluny III design;
Note the rounded apsidal chapels and processional aisles

To a large extent, these liturgical changes were influenced by, and derived from, the 11th century Cluniac reforms, as exemplified at St Etienne in Caen. Consequently, the buildings were designed to accommodate the new practices, especially the requirements of a large number of pilgrims. Architecturally, the most noticeable of these changes were at the east end of the churches. The complex design of this area contrasted with the simpler Saxon model.

1. Burton, Janet. *Monastic and Religious Orders in Britain 1000 to 1300.* 1994
2. Thompson, M W. *Associated Monasteries and Castles ... Archaeological Journal* 143 1986 p305-321

The focal points for these pilgrims would be the precious relic, more usually a collection of relics, housed behind the high altar at the east end, and the various shrines around the church, or raised high on a screen, such as the pulpitum at the entrance to the choir.[1] The pilgrims would normally enter through the northerly door of the west front into the north aisle, make their way round the church, circulating in a 'one way system', passing side-altars and shrines to various saints, and move round behind the altar, leaving their votive donations and offering their prayers. They left though the exit to the opposite aisle to the one they had entered by, that is by the south door at the west end of the church.

The 'sins' mentioned in the *Charter* may refer to the resistance by many of the Saxon clerical hierarchy to the new rulers, to the new liturgy and to the new buildings. Many are the examples around us today of parish churches which retain an element of their Saxon origins but which are largely post-Conquest. If we look at the great cathedrals and abbeys, we are hard pressed to discover complete pre-Norman examples.[2] Indeed, not only were their Saxon predecessors destroyed but the new buildings were placed largely over, or, as at Winchester, close to, the old. Could this have happened at Reading?

Once again, we need to look at Reading's two main ecclesiastical sites, St Mary's and the Forbury. In both cases there are arguments for the existence of Saxon churches at these locations. Also in both cases, the town now has post-Conquest ecclesiastical buildings.

The Crest of Reading Abbey

Finally, it is worth revisiting the sentence in the *Foundation Charter* which makes reference to the abbeys being destroyed on *account of sins*. If we omit the word *their,* then the 'sins' referred to may be those of perpetrators of the destruction rather than being attributed to the religious establishments themselves. This would certainly be consistent with the events at Leominster. If we include the word *their* it could, of course, refer to the Saxon hierarchy who resisted the newly appointed Norman clerics.

It is clear that Henry had been planning a new monastery which would house a variety of relics. He had been collecting these for some time before planning Reading Abbey. His new monastery was designed along the reformist Cluniac

1. See Mullaney J. *The Nave of Reading Abbey* www.readingabbeyhistory.com and
https://drive.google.com/file/d/1_COHBQ_oUX22boIn9JzXgq3SLrKyU_jv/view?usp=sharing
2. Taylor, HM. *Anglo-Saxon Architecture* 1965. (Updated 2015). Of the 400 or so churches with Saxon elements only St Laurence, Bradford on Avon is listed as *complete. http://www.anglo-saxon-churches.co.uk/*

model. Pilgrimage, along with the Benedictine tradition of welcoming travellers and strangers, would be at its core. To ensure its financial success it was granted extensive lands and income, and freed from the burden of taxation. The founding community were Cluniac monks. The first head of the newly formed community at Reading was Peter, the Prior of Cluny. He brought seven monks with him, and more joined him from the main Cluniac house in England, the Priory of St Pancras at Lewes in Suffolk. The first Abbot, appointed in 1123, had been the Prior of Lewes and was a personal friend of Henry. This was Hugh of Amiens, a renowned scholar, who was widely held in great regard[1]

Henry's one legitimate daughter was Matilda, or Maud, Empress of the Holy Roman Empire. On the death of her husband, the Emperor Henry V, in 1125, she returned to England with the Hand of St James. This was added to the relics held at Reading. It became the most important in its vast collection. Reading would from this time on be associated with St James, one of the principal saints of Christian pilgrimage, and his symbol, the scallop shell, would appear on the Abbey's coat of arms.

In 1288 the abbots of Reading were granted the right to use the mitre, ring, gloves, dalmatic, tunicle and sandals of a mitred abbot. They also sat in Parliament and were ranked highly in the Parliamentary writs. For instance, at the *Remembrance* of Henry VII's Queen, Elizabeth, the Abbot of Reading was ranked first. On another roll, at the time of Henry VIII, he was placed 10th.[2]

Following the building of the monastery in 1121, the town of Reading itself underwent a dramatic transformation. A new church, St Laurence's, was built to serve the townspeople. Towards the end of the century, St Laurence's was doubled in size, and a purpose built pilgrim house, or Hospitium, comprising a large reception hall. or refectory, and a dormitory, was built. This was named after St John the Baptist.

A small community of men and women was established and housed in buildings between the Hospitium and the church of St Laurence. They helped care for the pilgrims.[3]

The Abbey church itself was one of the largest in the country at the time, and the Abbey became a centre of government on several occasions, especially in the mid 15th century, when Parliament met there owing to outbreaks of plague in London. By the time of the Reformation, and its Dissolution in 1539, the Abbey

---

1. Mullaney L. *Henry I and His Abbey*.
2. Hurry, J. Reading Abbey p66. Hurry quotes the various sources
3. Mullaney, J. *RAQ* Part 4 Ch. 2.

was one of the richest in England, with an income in excess of £2000 per annum.[1]

The right of the Abbey to mint coin of the realm was retained and, although Edward II withdrew the right, this was short-lived, and by the time of Edward III it had been restored. It is probable that the actual mint was in London, though coins were attributed to Reading. Although examples are rare, those that do survive show the scallop shell on the reverse, set within a cross.

The town, with its main thoroughfares and churches as we know it today, was laid out by the Abbey. So too were its main market areas at Market Place and around St Mary's Butts. Its main river crossing, Caversham Bridge, leading to Oxford and the north, was the work of the Abbey. Even Reading's administrative structure evolved from the Town Guild, which was initially controlled by the Abbey. The Abbot chose a 'mayor' or *custos gilde,* from three nominees selected by the Guild members. The Guild eventually became the Corporation and later the Borough Council. From this, the town's industrial base grew. Reading's wealth was based on wool and associated trades.

A school was founded in the late 15th century in the Hospitium buildings. It has been argued that there may have been a town school even before this date. As times changed, pilgrimage became less popular, and the money was transferred from the upkeep of the Hospitium to sustaining a grammar school. This lasted until the middle of the 19th century and was the forerunner of Reading School.

In 1539 the townspeople appear to have turned their backs on the Abbey and preferred to have St Laurence's as their Parish Church, rather than the Abbey. Following its Dissolution the Abbey buildings were used as a quarry, both official and unofficial.

True, each monarch of the day did visit Reading, up to, and including, Charles I, but the Abbey was then left to decay until the 19th century.

Even the burial place of one of England's greatest kings, and most certainly the founder of Reading as we know it today, Henry I, was forgotten and possibly destroyed.

---

1. *Valor ecclesiasticus 1535.* This was a general assessment of church property undertaken by Henry VIII following the *Act of Supremacy* and his break with Rome. As Head of the Church, he wished to know the true value of his newly acquired property.

CONCLUSION

Today's inhabitants of Reading are the successors of all those peoples whom we have met in the pages of this book. Two thousand years ago Calleva was the largest town in the area. It was the commercial, military and transport hub for central southern Britain. It was also a town not just of locals, but of immigrants who came from all over the known world.

About fifteen hundred years ago, Reading replaced Calleva as this centre. Like Calleva, it is a town both of immigrants and of those born locally. Some of the latter can trace their ancestry back many generations; some may even carry the genes of those early Celts, Saxons or Romans. Most, however, will be newcomers to this area, if not to this country.[1]

Even the name of the town itself reflects this intermingling, not just of peoples, but of its journey through time.

All its inhabitants, past, present and future, share in the ever-evolving story of Reading and look to that small triangle of raised land that lies between the rivers Kennet and Thames, and call it home.

And finally, can we say for certain why Henry I decided upon Reading for his monastery and mausoleum?

We can probably not better the reasons given by his contemporary, the chronicler William of Malmesbury who wrote,

> *He built this monastery between the river Kennet and the Thames,*
> *in a place calculated for the reception of almost all who might*
> *have occasion to travel to the most populous cities of England.*[2]

I hope this book helps us understand the long history of the two towns and their peoples, all of which combined to make Reading this important place, extolled by Malmesbury, and chosen by Henry for his great abbey and mausoleum.

---

1. See Appendix B page 119-120.

2. William of Malmesbury, *Gesta regum anglorum* Vol 2 Bk 5 p413.

Hoc ille coenobium inter duo flumina Kenetam et Tamensem constituit, loco ubi pene omnium itinerantium ad populosiores urbes Angliae posset esse diversorium.

The Latin word *diversorium,* translated as 'calculated for the reception of', more accurately means a 'lodging place'. Could this indicates that Reading already had a tourist industry, with a a major place, or places to stay, even before the monastery was founded in 1121?

APPENDIX A

DEATH OF STILICO   Zosimus Bk 5 159 –162

This translation of Zosimus' *New History* was printed in 1814
by W. Green and T. Chaplin in London.

Stilicho was therefore filled with anxiety concerning these circumstances. The Barbarians, who were with him, were very desirous of putting in force their former plan, and so endeavoured to dissuade him from the measures which he now wished to adopt. But being unable to prevail with him, they all determined to remain elsewhere, until they should be better apprized of the emperor's sentiments towards Stilico.

However Sarus excelled all the other confederates in power and rank, and accompanied by the Barbarians under his command, killed all the Huns who formed Stilico's guard while they were asleep. Sarus also seized all the carriages in Stilico's camp, entered his tent, and remained to observe how the situation would unfold.

Upon this Stilico, observing that his Barbarians were quarrelling among themselves, hastened to Ravenna, and took control of the cities where there were any women or children belonging to the Barbarians. This was to prevent them from occupying these towns.

In the meantime Olympius, who was now become the Emperor's chief advisor, sent the imperial mandate to the soldiers at Ravenna, ordering them immediately to apprehend Stilico, and to detain him in prison without fetters. When Stilico heard this, while it was night, he took refuge in a nearby Christian church. Seeing this his Barbarians, with their families, followers and servants, were all armed and were ready for what would ensue.

When day appeared, Sarus' soldiers, entered the church and swore before the bishop, that they were commanded by the Emperor not to kill Stilico, but to keep him in custody. Being brought out of the church, and once in the custody of the soldiers, another letter was produced by the same messenger who had brought the first, in which the punishment of death was proclaimed against Stilico, for his crimes against the commonwealth.

So, while Eucherius, his son, fled towards Rome, Stilico was led to execution. The Barbarians in his retinue, along with his servants and other friends and relations, of whom there was a vast number, resolved to rescue him. But Stilico forbade them, threatening them with punishment should they attempt this. He calmly submitted his neck to the sword.

Stilico was the most moderate and just of all the men who possessed great authority in his time, For although he was married to the niece of the Theodosius Ist, was entrusted with the empires of both his sons, and had been the Imperial Commander for twenty-three years, he never conferred military rank for money, or coveted the stipend of the soldiers to his own use.

Being the father of only one son, he offered to him office of Tribune of the Notarii, and encouraged him neither to desire nor to attempt to obtain any other office or authority.

In order that no studious person, or astrologers, may be ignorant of the time of his death, I shall relate that it happened in the consulship of Bassus and Philippus, during which the Emperor Arcadius submitted to his fate, on the twenty-second day of August.

APPENDIX B

DNA

It seems that almost daily advances are being announced in what we may loosely call DNA technology to identify the ancestry of the inhabitants of Britain. The following is one such excerpt reported in *Current Archaeology,* March 2016.

The first whole genome sequences in this study were created using human remains excavated at Oakington near Cambridge. As the article reported, it sheds *a new light on the impact of Anglo-Saxon migration to this country.* In broad terms the Anglo–Saxon immigrants contributed about 38% of the DNA of modern inhabitants of eastern England and 30% to Welsh and Scottish populations.

Rarecoal analysis.

A new framework called 'rarecoal' is used to calculate the joint allele frequency spectrum across multiple populations using rare alleles. (An allele is one of a number of alternative forms of the same gene or same genetic locus)

Findings

The following are excerpts from the report, which should be referred to in full.

British population history has been shaped by a series of immigrations, including the early Anglo-Saxon migrations after 400 CE. It remains an open question how these events affected the genetic composition of the current British population. Here, we present whole-genome sequences from 10 individuals excavated close to Cambridge in the East of England, ranging from the late Iron Age to the middle Anglo-Saxon period. By analysing shared rare variants with hundreds of modern samples from Britain and Europe, we estimate that on average the contemporary East English population derives 38% of its ancestry from Anglo-Saxon migrations. We gain further insight with a new method, rarecoal, which infers population history and identifies fine-scale genetic ancestry from rare variants. Using rarecoal we find that the Anglo-Saxon samples are closely related to modern Dutch and Danish populations, while the Iron Age samples share ancestors with multiple Northern European populations including Britain.

Up to this point we have interpreted the genetic structure of the Anglo-Saxon samples in terms of recent immigrant versus indigenous populations. However, in the absence of a time series through the Romano-British period from the Iron Age to the Anglo-Saxon period, we should also consider the possibility that some of the genetic heterogeneity seen in the Oakington samples arose earlier due to immigration in Romano-British times.

For Roman immigration patterns to generate this diverse structure in the fifth to sixth century Oakington samples, one would have to assume strong social segregation with little interbreeding over multiple generations. This seems unlikely given that immigration into Roman-Britain was geographically diverse and consisted of an administrative elite and the military, who would have interbred and recruited locally, particularly in the last decades of the third and fourth centuries.

Appendices

Furthermore, there is no significant Roman settlement at Oakington and no evidence for significant Roman Heritage

Given the mixing apparent c.500 CE, and that the modern population is not more than 40% of Anglo -Saxon ancestry, it is perhaps surprising that the middle Anglo-Saxon individuals from the more dispersed field cemetery in Hinxton look more genetically consistent with unmixed immigrant ancestry. One possibility is that this reflects continued immigration until at least the Middle Saxon period. The unmixed Hinxton group, versus the mixing of the Oakington population, shows that early medieval migration took a variety of forms and that these migrants integrated with the incumbent population in different ways. Full-genome sequences, and new methods such as rarecoal, now allow us to use slight distinctions in genetic ancestry to study such recent events. Further ancient genomes, and methodological improvements to incorporate explicit migration and mixing, will enable us to resolve them in more detail.

We saw, on pages 98-99, that the isotope analysis at Berinsfield, which indicated only 5.3% of the skeletal samples originated from continental Europe, supporting, as the report says *the hypothesis of acculturation.*

Comment

The science in this field is developing rapidly and with further developments no doubt will come new, and probably different, statistics and theories.

Maps and chart showing gene origins and distribution for England with specific reference to Hinxton

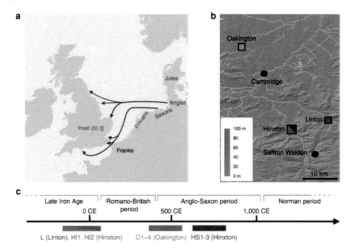

Sources and Acknowledgements

Current Archaeology March 2016 reporting on *Nature Communications 7 Article 10408* January 2016 Title: Iron Age and Anglo-Saxon genomes from East England reveal British migration history http://www.nature.com/ncomms/2016/160119/ncomms10408/full/ncomms10408.html

Current Archaeology September 2020. *Who did the Anglo-Saxons think they were?* This mentions DNA research into the nature and origins of the Anglo-Saxon peoples.

APPENDIX C

The Anglo-Saxon Chronicle 871

The Danish Viking army in Reading, from the Anglo-Saxon Chronicle

Appendices

APPENDIX D

THE NOTITIA DIGNITATUM

The *Notitia Dignitatum* is an enigmatic document describing the bureaucracy of fifth-century Britain. It is also the main piece of evidence of the term *Litoris Saxonici* (Saxon Shore). Though we speak mostly of the *Notitia Dignitatum*, the real title of this manuscript is *Notitia omnium Dignitatum et administrationum tam civilium quam militarum*, an official list of civil and military offices in the western empire, which was of service to the *primicerius notariorum occidentis* (imperial records office of the West), which kept records of all imperial administrative affairs

Below is a list of the offices and troops for Britain. The chapters represent the Western part of the Empire. This is abbreviated to *Occ* in the *Notitia*. This list is incomplete as to the units stationed in Britain, their number representing a rough guide to dates of their creation, or upgrade from the *limitanei* into the *comitatenses* or degradation to a lower status.

The copies we have date only to the 15th and 16th centuries. These are based on an 11th century copy, the *Codex Spirensis,* now lost. Most scholars consider these to be a fairly accurate representations of the original, but a degree of caution is required. There is some consensus that the *Notitia* was drawn up under Stilicho. This is based on the fact that the *Notitia* is in fact two documents, covering the two parts of the Empire, but drawn up for the specific purposes of one ruler who had in mind to govern both halves separately. The argument goes that this fits Stilicho's ambition to control both parts of the Empire after the death of Arcadius in 408.

NOTITIA DIGNITATUM OCCIDENTIS	REGISTER OF WESTERN DIGNITARIES
Vicarii *VI:* *Vicarius Britanniae*	Six **vicars**: … of the Britains.
Comites rei militaris *VI:* *Comes Britanniarum* *Comes Litoris Soxonicum per Britannias*	Six **military counts**: … of the Britains; of the Saxon shore of (for) the Britains.
Duces *XIII:* *Dux Britanniarum*	Thirteen **dukes**: … of the Britains
Consularii *XXII:* *Britanniae II:* *Consularis per Maxima Caesariensis* *Consularis per Valentia*	Twenty-two **consulars**: in the Britains two: of Maxima Caesariensis, of Valentia.
Presidii *XXXI:* *Britanniae III:* *Praesidis per Britannia prima* *Praesidis per Britannia secunda* *Praesidis per Flavia Caesariensis*	Thirty-one **presidents**: in the Britains three: President of Britain 1 President of Britain 2 President of Flavia Caesariensis

Page from the *Notitia Dignitatum*

Ref PhD Thesis Ruth O'Hara *An Assessment of the Notitia Dignitatum as a Historical Source for the Late Roman Bureaucracy* Maynooth 2013

APPENDIX E

AETHELFLAEDE'S WILL

Aethelflaed was the daughter of Ealdorman Aelfgar and the second wife of King Edmund, whose first wife died in 946.

þis is Æthelflede cwyde. is ærst ic gean minum hlaforde þes landes æt Lmaburnan þæs æt Ceolsige æt Readingan.

This is Aethelflaed's will. First I grant to my lord the estate at Lambourn, those at Cholsey (and) at Reading.

THE STRUCTURE OF THE WESTERN ROMAN EMPIRE C 395AD

The Prefecture of Gaul (red)

This prefecture was divided into three Dioceses; Spain, Gaul and Britain.

The Diocese of Britain (see page 56)

This was divided into five **Provinces**

Maxima Caesariensis, Valentia, Britannia I, Britannia II
Flavia Caesariensis

The **Prefecture of Italy (yellow)**

The **Prefecture of Illyricum (dark green)**

Territories outside either the Eastern or Western Empire (light green)

This above listing is from the *Notitia Dignitatum.*

© https://en.wikipedia.org/wiki/Praetorian_prefecture_of_Italy#/media/
File:Praetorian_Prefectures_of_the_Roman_Empire_395_AD.png with name additions jgmullaney

INDEX OF PEOPLE AND TRIBES

('f' after an entry means the reference is in a footnote) Saxon initial Æ and Ae are not differentiated and may be abbrevaietd to 'E' in the text)

Index of people and tribes

Index of people and tribes

BIBLIOGRAPHY

Some of the following occur in the other indices. This is a list showing the pages where the bibliographical sources are mentioned. The abbreviation 'f' signifies that the reference is in a footnote.

Astill, G. Historic Towns in Berkshire 42 42f 89f 157

Bayley, M. 85f 107
Berisford and Brown. 84
Bertram, forgery of the Itinerarium Antonini Augusti 37
Blinkhorn, P. 75
Boon, G. Silchester: the Roman town of Calleva 15 15f 16 16f 23 23f 30f 31f 32f 59f 107
Brooke, G.C. 99

Chandler, J. A Higher Reality   96f 138
Creighton, J. Coins and power in Late Iron Age Britain, 22 22f 25f 138
Cunliffe, B. 33

Dolley, R. H. M. A Note on the Anglo-Saxon Mint of Reading   99 99f 138
Doran, J. The History and Antiquities of the Town and Borough of Reading in Berkshire 85 85f 138

Farrer, W. An Outline Itinerary of King Henry the First. 106f 138
Fox, A 23 31f
Freeman, A. Reading: Its Status and Standing as a Minor Late Anglo-Saxon Mint. 99 99f 101 101f
Frere, S. Britannia 28f 32 32f 47f 49 49f 56 56f 61f 63f 65 65f 66f 138
Fulford, M. 15f 24f 30f 32f 137

Gelling, M. Place Names of Berkshire   91 92f 138
Giles, J.A. William of Malmesbury's Chronicle 107f 138

Green, A. 72 138
Green, J. 106 138

Hardman, P. vi 89
Haskins. 108
Hawkes and Fasham. 42 42f 75f 77f
Hollister, Warrren. Henry I 105f 106f 108 139
Hughes, Susan S. 99f
Hurry, J. The History of Reading Abbey   97 97f 104f 114f 138

Jervis. B. 75f

Bibliography

Kemp, B. The Reading Abbey Cartularies iii 92 92f 104 104f 105f 110 110f
Kerry, C. Transactions of the Berkshire Archaeological & Architectural Society and A history of the municipal church of St Laurence, Reading, 1883. 90f 91f 97 97f 98
Kift, M. Life in Old Caversham 93f 138

Margary, I. The Roman Roads in Britain   37f 39 39f 40 41 138
Mullaney, J. Reading's Abbey Quarter 79f 113f 114f 137

Oppenheimer, S.   19f 85 85f 139
Over, L. 15f 35f 37f 139

Pearman, M.T. 93

Ravenscroft, W. The Discovery of Human Remains in the Forbury, Reading . 98 98f 137
Reynolds, T. 34f 139

Slade, C. iii 8 8f 34 35 35f 42 42f 79 79f 80 80f 81-83 83f 84 89 95 97 97f 98 98f 99 108 137

Taylor, H.M. Anglo-Saxon Architecture 113f 139
Timby, J. 30f 137

Underwood, C. 75f

Wacher, John. 23f 26f 31f 32f 33 33f 60f 66f 69f 138 139
Wessex Archaeology 42 42f 77f
Wing, W. 93
Wykes, A. 85 85f 87 92f 139

SOURCES

Primary Sources.

Asserius Menevensis (Known as Asser) *De rebus gestis Aelfredi*

Bede *Historia ecclesiastica gentis Anglorum*

Caesar / Hirtius *Commentarii de Bello Gallico*
Cassius Dio *Roman History (Ρωμαϊκὴ Ἱστορία, Historia Romana)*
Chronica Gallica
Claudian *De Bello Gothico*
Claudian *De consulatu Stilichonis*
Claudian *De consulatu Stilichonis*
Claudian *In Eutropium*

Domesday Book   (Phillimore edition 1979)

Foundation Charter of Reading Abbey 1125. Reading Abbey Cartularies ed Kemp

Gaius *Institutiones*
Gildas *De excidio*

Hydatius. *Chronica minora*

John of Worcester *Chronicle*

Leland, John. *Cygnea cantio*.
Liber Vitae. Register and Martyrology of New Minster and Hyde Abbey, ed. W. de Gray
    Birch (Hampshire Record Society), 1892

Notitia Dignitatum

Ordericus Vitalis. *Historia Ecclesiastica*

Procopius. *History of the Wars, Bk 3* The Project Gutenberg eBook, History of the Wars,
    Books III and IV (of 8), Translated by H. B. Dewing

Sextus Julius Frontinus *Strategemata*

Tacitus *Agricola* and   *Annals*

Valor ecclesiasticus 1535

William of Malmesbury (edition Roffensis in the appendix).

Zosimus (Zozimos – Greek Ζώσιμος) *Historia Nova* (Ἱστορία Νέα, "New History")

Archaeological Sources

Berrisford, F. *The Anglo-Saxon Pottery* in *Excavations at Shakenoak*
Bradley, R and Richards, J. *Excavation of Two Ring Ditches at Heron's House, Burghfield.*
    BAJ 70
Brown and Avery, *The Pottery and other Finds in Saxon Features at Abingdon:* Oxoniensa

Sources

Cowell, R.W. Fulford, M.G. & Lobb, S. *Excavations of Prehistoric and Roman Settlements at Aldermaston Wharf.* BAJ 69

Fulford, M. 1984. *Silchester: Excavations on the Defences 1974-80.* London: Society for Antiquaries. Britannia Monograph Series No. 5

Fulford, M. and Timby, J. 2000. *Late Iron Age and Roman Silchester: Excavations on the Site of the Forum Basilica*, 1977, 1980-86. London

Mullaney, J. *The Nave of Reading Abbey* *www.readingabbeyhistory.com*

Oxford Archaeology job no. 3195 *Minster of St Mary the Virgin. Watching brief. 2006*

Ravenscroft, W. *The Discovery of Human Remains in the Forbury, Reading.* BAJ 13 1907

Seaby, W A, *A Romano-British Building at Knowl Hill, Berks.* BAJ 36, 1932.
Seaby, W A. *Some Pre-Roman Remains from South Reading.* BAJ 36. 1932
Slade, C. *Excavation at Reading Abbey 1971-1973* BAJ Vol 68
Stevens J. *Discovery of an Ancient Cemetery in Reading.* BAJ 1895 Journal 1

Thames Valley Archaeological Services 2014. *Rear of 7-9 Gun Street.*
The Thames through Time; The Archaeology of the Gravel Terraces of the Upper and Middle Thames, Oxford Archaeology. 2009

Wilson, D G. *The Making of the Middle Thames* p26.

Secondary Sources and Commentaries

Abels, R. *English Logistics and military administration*
Astill, G.G. *Historic Towns in Berkshire: An Archaeological Appraisal.* 1978

Bayley, M. *Celtic Place Names.*
Boon, G. *Roman Silchester*
Boon, G. *Silchester, the Roman Town of Calleva*
Burton, J. *Monastic and Religious Orders in Britain 1000 to 1300.* 1994

Chandler, J. *A Higher Reality*
Coates, R. *Invisible Britons: The view from linguistics.* Paper circulated in connection with the conference *Britons and Saxons*, 14–16 April. University of Sussex Linguistics and English Language Department.(2004)
Creighton, J. *Coins and power in Late Iron Age Britain*, Cambridge University Press, 2000.

Dils, J. *Reading a history*
Dolley, R H M. *A Note on the Anglo-Saxon Mint of Reading*
Doran, J. *The History and Antiquities of the Town and Borough of Reading in Berkshire* 1835

Farrer, W. *An Outline Itinerary of King Henry the First.* 1919
Fox, A. *Anitiquity xxii* 1948, quoted by Wacher, John, in *The Towns of Roman Britain*

Frere, S. *Britannia*
Fulford, M. *City of the Dead: Calleva Atrebatum.*

Gelling M. *Place Names of Berkshire*
Giles, J.A. *William of Malmesbury's Chronicle.* 1847
Good, V L. *The Most Ancient Church of Reading. 1970*
Green, A. "The Last Century of Danegeld", *The English Historical Review* 96
Green, J. *Henry I.* 2009
Guy, C. *Roman Circular Lead Tanks in Britain.* Britannia XII 1981.

Hollister, W. *Henry I*
Henig, M. *Togidubnus and the Roman liberation* British Archaeology 37 Sept 1998.
Historical Notes on the Parish Church of St Mary the Virgin 1914 (Reading Library).
Hurry, J. *Reading Abbey* (1901)

Kerry C. *A history of the municipal church of St Laurence, Reading.* 1883.
Kerry C. *Transactions of the Berkshire Archaeological & Architectural Society : papers
        read before the Society during the session, 1880-1.*
Kift, M. *Life in Old Caversham*

Margary I. *The Roman Roads in Britain*
Matthews, J. *Western Aristocracies and Imperial Court AD 364–425*
Moorhead, S. and Stuttard, D. *AD 410 The Year that Shook Rome*

Oppenheimer, S. *The Origins of the British* (2006),
Over L. *Roman Villa Settlement in the Middle Thames Valley* 1970

Reynolds T. *Iter Britannarium*

Salway, P. *Roman Britain* and his *Tom Hassall Lecture 1977, 'Roman Oxfordshire'*
Slade, C. *Historic Towns*
Stenton, F M. *The Early History of the Abbey of Abingdon*

Taylor, HM. *Anglo-Saxon Architecture* 1965. (Updated 2015).
Thompson, M W. *Associated Monasteries and Castles ... Archaeological Journal* 143 1986

Vainyte, G. *Roman Law, Roman Citizenship, Roman Identity* .
Victoria County Histories, Wiltshire Vol 9

Wacher, J. *The Towns of Roman Britain*
Whitelock, D. *Anglo-Saxon Wills "aet Readingum".*
Wykes, A. *Reading—A Biography.* 1970

Yorke, B. *Wessex in the Early Middle Ages*

Scallop Shell Press

Ever since the Middle Ages the scallop shell has been the symbol of those going on pilgrimage to the shrine of St James in Compostela, Spain.

The shell became a metaphor for the journey, the grooves representing the many ways of arriving at one's destination.   At a practical level the shell was also useful for scooping up water to drink or food to eat.

Today the pilgrimage is even more popular than ever as people of all faiths, and none, seek a meaning for their journey through life.

Scallop Shell Press aims to publish works which, like the grooves of the shell, will offer the modern pilgrim stories of our shared humanity and help readers arrive at their own meaningful interpretations of life. We hope that our books will be shells within whose covers readers will find an intellectual and spiritual source of sustenance for their own personal pilgrimages.

Other published titles

Early Closing Day, Air Raids on Reading 1939-1945, Mike Cooper

Hugh Cook Faringdon, The Last Abbot of Reading, Chris Darbyshire

Reformation, Revolution and Rebirth, The Story if the Return of Catholicism to Reading and the Founding of St James' Parish, John Mullaney and Lindsay Mullaney

The Reading Abbey Stone, John Mullaney

The Stained Glass of St James' Church Reading, John Mullaney

The Timms Family of Reading and London, Katie Amos

Views from the Hill, The Story of Whitley, Dennis Wood

Forthcoming

Henry I and his Abbey, Lindsay Mullaney

If you would like to find out more about Scallop Shell Press visit our website

www.Scallopshellpress.co.uk